T0313276

Business Transformation Planning for Leaders

A Tactical Roadmap for Achieving Profitable Growth with the Highest Return on Capital

Business Transformation Planning for Leaders

A Tactical Roadmap for Achieving Profitable Growth with the Highest Return on Capital

By
Kiran Gurumurthy

A PRODUCTIVITY PRESS BOOK

First edition published in 2019
by Routledge/Productivity Press
52 Vanderbilt Ave. New York, NY 10017, USA
2 Park Square, Milton Park, Abingdon, Oxon OX14 4RN, UK

International Standard Book Number-13: 978-1-138-37066-1 (Hardback)
International Standard Book Number-13: 978-0-429-42790-9 (eBook)

Library of Congress Cataloging-in-Publication Data

Names: Gurumurthy, Kiran, author.
Title: Business transformation planning for leaders : a tactical roadmap for achieving profitable growth with the highest return on capital / Kiran Gurumurthy.
Description: 1 Edition. | New York : Taylor & Francis, [2019] | Includes bibliographical references and index.
Identifiers: LCCN 2018038424 (print) | LCCN 2018051467 (ebook) | ISBN 9780429427909 (e-Book) | ISBN 9781138370661 (hardback : alk. paper)
Subjects: LCSH: Organizational change. | Organizational effectiveness. | Organizational change. | Strategic planning. | Leadership.
Classification: LCC HD58.8 (ebook) | LCC HD58.8 .G866 2019 (print) | DDC 658.4/063--dc23
LC record available at https://lccn.loc.gov/2018038424

Visit the Taylor & Francis Web site at
http://www.taylorandfrancis.com

Contents

About the Author..vii

Chapter 1 Introduction 1

Chapter 2 Case Study Company Overview..7

Chapter 3 Business Performance: Secret Ingredients 11

Chapter 4 Revenue Growth: The Elusive Unicorn 15

　　　Volume 19
　　　　　1. Identify High-Growth Market Segments......................19
　　　　　2. Understand the Needs of the High-Growth
　　　　　Market Segments 21
　　　　　3. Understand the Current Performance to Meet the
　　　　　Needs of the High-Growth Market Segments...................23
　　　　　4. Develop an Action Plan to Grow the Volume 24
　　　Pricing 26
　　　　　1. Eliminating Unfavorable Outliers...............................26
　　　　　2. Pricing Existing Products for Value............................. 28
　　　　　3. New Products Pricing 30
　　　　　4. Improving Pricing Execution 30
　　　Summary 32
　　　Product Mix.. 34

Chapter 5 Cost Optimization: Crack the Nut without Creating
　　　a Mess... 39

　　　1. Understand the Cost Drivers 40
　　　2. Identify and Eliminate Noncore Costs............................. 43
　　　3. Optimize Core Costs..47

Chapter 6 Working Capital: The Right Grade of Fuel 59

    Inventory.. 60
        1. Categorize Inventory Levels Over Time......................61
        2. Segment Inventory Based on Variability of
          Demand and Inventory Value......................................62
        3. Develop Inventory Management Strategy for
          Each Segment 65
        4. Identify Inventory Stocking Levels 67
    Summary 69
    Accounts Receivable..70
        1. Improved Execution 71
        2. Accounts Receivable Cycle Management 73
        3. Accounts Receivable Terms Rationalization.............75
        4. Technology Upgrades...76
    Summary 76
    Accounts Payable 77
    Summary 77

Chapter 7 Execution Plan: Operating Rules 81

        1. Talent Selection 81
        2. Operating Behaviors..82
        3. Operating Cadence 83

Chapter 8 Summary... 87

Index.. 91

About the Author

Kiran Gurumurthy is a senior business executive who has led business turnarounds in multiple industries. He has driven significant improvements in both public and private equity space.

Kiran's strength—being able to look at complex problems, simplify them, and then engage others to solve them—has been the secret to his success. Kiran is leveraging this strength to document his lessons learned at various companies into simple content for readers to learn and develop their skills. Over the course of his career, Kiran has always trained and developed others along the way. This development of people has given him the confidence to document his approach and share with others. Over the course of the next few years, Kiran plans to write books related to business transformation, pricing, global supply chain management, global footprint optimization, establishing centers of excellence, and talent identification and development.

Kiran has held various roles and is currently the vice president of operations and supply chain for an $8 billion Fortune 500 company. He is well connected to senior business leaders across the globe. Kiran's educational background includes having earned an MBA, an MS (Industrial Engineering), and a BS (Mechanical Engineering). He is a certified Six Sigma Master Black Belt and Lean expert.

1

Introduction

A rapidly changing business environment, higher expectations of results, and limited resources are impeding businesses from blooming. A business is a complex web of factors that requires systematic understanding to be successful. The factors that determine business success are in a constant state of flux. Varied needs by multiple channels, changing customer buying behaviors, commodity price fluctuations, foreign exchange impact, technology, and globalization are some of the obstacles that corporations have to overcome. Research in Motion (RIM), popularly known as Blackberry, was once a success story and the darling of Wall Street. But the company's market share fell from 20% to 0.1% in less than 7 years. This drop in sales was primarily due to changing business factors, such as consumer buying behavior, competitor actions, evolution of technology, execution, and so forth. Due to the inability of RIM to transform, the company got into losses, had to lay off thousands of employees, and was sold to a private firm.

Despite the above operating hurdles, the expectations of results from shareholders are ever increasing. Shareholder activism over the last couple of decades is significantly impacting the pressures of running a business. Mergers and acquisitions (M&A) are also fueling higher stress on business leaders to provide higher returns, since the valuation of the deals needs to be justified with limited resources. The justification of acquisitions usually refers to significant synergy benefits on an expedited timeline. Business leaders who are required to lead in roles such as chief executive officer (CEO), chief operating officer (COO), president, vice president, general manager, and director are more challenged than ever. The average tenure of CEOs has been decreasing due to these demanding expectations. Also, the time required to fill these key leadership roles is longer than ever.

Business transformation is not a one-time event. When a company transforms, competitors react and markets adapt. As a result, companies need to constantly keep evolving or transforming to gain an edge in the marketplace. When Dell Computers started offering computers in a direct-to-consumer model, customers could get their computers faster and at a lower cost. That transformation provided Dell a competitive edge in the marketplace. However, in a few years, other companies started doing the same and customer expectations for lead time had been reset. Dell Computers lost the edge and got into financial trouble. Hence, business transformations are a continuous process that need to keep evolving. Companies that can develop the competency of driving transformations consistently can succeed over the long term.

Who should read this book? This book is for business leaders who have responsibility for the success of the profit and loss (P&L) statement of a business. The specific titles of the P&L leader may vary by company or industry. This book provides a roadmap for the business leader to develop a comprehensive business transformation plan. A plan that is simple, fact based, and actionable. This book is also a guide for professionals aspiring to be future P&L leaders. Human resources department leaders can provide this roadmap to budding business leaders and see how they consistently execute to develop the talent pipeline. The holistic cross-functional and general manager view of a business that is taken in this book is useful for all department heads. For example, a sales leader reading this book can understand why running a promotion to drive sales without understanding the capacity of supply chain can actually result in losing customers. The case study methodology used to illustrate the concepts makes the material easy to read and easy to relate to practical application by readers in their companies. Additionally, business leaders responsible for due diligence and integration to create value in M&A can use the approach explained in this book.

One of the challenges that the P&L leader responsible for the transformation faces is experience bias. A business leader with a marketing background tends to look for ways to revive the company's performance through marketing activities such as strategic planning, product positioning, and advertising. The problem with this approach is that a business is a labyrinth of cross-functional activities; therefore, narrowing in on only one area does not provide the expected results. Sometimes forcing all the efforts in an area of comfort for the business leader hides the real challenges of the business and the problem only gets worse with time. Hence, the cross-functional and holistic approach shown in this book produces a better business transformation plan.

You will notice that the book is written from a very practical point of view. You will not see a lot of theoretical and academic discussions. Extensive data and statistical analysis are not the goal of this book. A huge research or strategy department is not needed to conduct the analysis mentioned in this book. The approach shown in it is a very practical and commonsense roadmap to achieve profitable growth for any business. There are no corporate mantras and consulting jargons that have become commonplace in today's businesses. A series of questions are asked to arrive at the answers. Overdemanding business leaders and "corporate superheroes" (business firefighters) cannot provide sustainable results to a company. Rather, a simple plan with all key players aligned can provide significant impact to the company's performance.

This book has been developed from the experience of personally leading several business transformations and inputs from various other business leaders from multiple industries. The concepts and approach discussed can be universally applied in all industries and companies of any scale. Though the case study company used for discussion is a manufacturing company, the approach could easily be applied in business services companies as well. The commonsense approach discussed is applicable for both for-profit and nonprofit organizations. A practical tips section is included in most chapters. These tips are based on the actual implementation experiences of several business leaders.

This book is also a practical alignment tool for a company undergoing transformation. The roadmap shown in this book is a great way to engage the management team of a business unit to understand and drive the business transformation. The management team can read the book, get together for a couple of days (preferably off-site), and discuss by chapter the lessons learned, how the chapter applies to their business, and what improvements they should focus on based on the learnings. Note that all changes may not be necessary for all companies. Based on data analysis and the situation of the business, the management team can determine the areas to focus on for improvement. The greatest outcome you can get from this book is to have an aligned team that is focused on common priorities to execute. By getting the management team to work through this thought process and identifying areas to focus on, you will ensure that they have ownership of the solutions. Having this ownership of actions is critical to keeping the team focused and willing to work harder. The roadmap shown can also be used for successfully integrating acquisitions made by a company to create value.

The business transformation plan that will be developed will be a great way to communicate and keep the whole organization focused. The transformation plan should be action oriented, time-bound, and linked to specific owners. It is very easy for the business to get distracted in doing several things that may amount to nothing. Remember, several changes may not make an impact at the company level. Hence, having a common transformation plan or blueprint becomes necessary to communicate and keep the organization focused. Can you imagine building a house without a blueprint or project plan that is communicated to all contractors? Have you ever seen a cabinet maker show up at the construction site during the foundation phase? No, this is because the blueprint developed along with project plan will let the cabinet maker know when he should be ready with his deliverables for completing the house on time. In the same way, the business transformation plan will keep all functions aligned and help support the achievement of a common goal.

How is the business transformation planning shown in this book different from other business improvement or continuous improvement approaches? The first difference is the process of developing the transformation plan. As you will see in the following chapters, this book provides insight on how to engage the entire company in developing this transformation plan so that the net impact of any changes can be understood across the company. Most companies have a quality improvement plan that may be developed by quality and operations functions, a business development plan that is created by the sales team, and so forth. However, there is no alignment, expectations of assistance needed from other functions, or clear understanding of the impact of their plans and actions across the company. Hence, expected results are either never achieved or delayed. Second, as you will see in this book, the shareholder expectations drive the growth strategy of the business, which is supported by the right cost optimization actions with the required capital investment to support the growth. Achieving this type of clearly aligned activities requires strategic thinking and a good roadmap, as shown in this book. Many companies start from a bottom-up grassroots improvement effort in a function and hope that everything they are doing meets the expectations of the top executives and shareholders. When the top executives and shareholders do not see these grassroots actions as top priority, the employees driving these actions get frustrated. This book shows how to start from the top and then ensure that the improvements derived across the company support the expectations from the top. The third difference is that the book shows how to "sell" your ideas and recommendations to senior executives. Many ideas in businesses do not get supported or implemented because the ideas are not presented in a simple and visual format that is easy for executives to absorb. When too much time is wasted on explaining the actions and results, senior executives tend to lose attention. However, if the data analysis is presented in a simple visual format, then it is easier to focus on the next steps. The charts presented in this book are very articulate in making the obvious conclusions. Finally, this book is different in its breadth and depth of addressing business improvement. There are several books available that present a lot of information about a particular subject or subjects. For example, there are books on pricing, marketing, working capital improvement, and so forth. But these books are not broad enough to address a holistic business transformation. They have depth of subject but lack breadth across the various functions. Also, unless you want to become an expert in pricing, why would you read a 400-page book on pricing and try to implement its strategies and yet not make any improvements in other parts of your business? So in order to get a broad understanding of business transformation, this is a great book.

For the sake of illustration, we will discuss a company called Case Study Company (CSC). This company is based in the United States and manufactures custom hardwood doors primarily for the North American market. As you explore through this journey at your organization, you will find your own variations to improve your business performance. The key is to get started by engaging a cross-functional team and exploring all the questions methodically; that will automatically lead toward a solid business transformation plan. Every company tends to think, "We are different." Yes, that may be true in terms of having a unique mix of value to the customer, geographic presence, team talent, business evolution, financial situation, and so forth. However, all businesses have common core elements, such as customers, value to customers, products or services portfolio, processes, and infrastructure, to execute value to customers. The transformation roadmap or thought process shown in this book is focused on understanding and improving the core elements of the business to provide sustainable business results. As you will see, the roadmap shown can be easily adapted to any business.

2

Case Study Company Overview

Business concepts are easier to understand when we can apply them to a company or problem that we are familiar with. For the purpose of illustration, we will select a company that produces a fairly simple product in North America. But as you will see from reading this book, the product or service could be more complex and the scope of the business could be global as well. For our case, we will discuss a hypothetical company that manufactures hardwood doors for residential use. The Case Study Company (CSC) is based in the United States. The customers are spread across North America. The company sells its products through distributors, wholesalers, builders, and big-box building supply stores. The company does not sell directly to homeowners.

The sales team for CSC engages in customer contact through regular visits, cold calling, trade shows, and referrals. Each salesman has a region based on the potential market size. For example, there is one salesman who covers Florida, Georgia, and South Carolina. And all of the Northwest is covered by one salesman. The customer service team in the office receives requests for quote (RFQs), processes them, and submits them back to the customers. The customer service team is also responsible for providing order status, ensuring that customer delivery performance is managed, and resolving any customer concerns.

The company has about 300 employees in its manufacturing facility and corporate office. The main factory has two computer numerical control (CNC) routers, four door machines, workstations for assembly work, two door-sizing machines, four sanding booths, and a paint booth for finishing the doors. The operations team in the factory consists of warehouse pickers, door machine operators, CNC operators, assemblers, sanders, painters, and logistics operators that manage shipping, receiving, and freight.

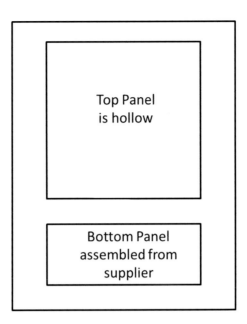

FIGURE 2.1
Door blank as received from suppliers.

The company also has a new warehouse on the West Coast, to support demand of West Coast builders, which employs about 20 employees.

CSC imports door blanks into the country. A door blank is a door without the top panel, hardware, weather strip, or any other work performed to it. A door blank is shown in Figure 2.1. The company only sells hardwood exterior doors. CSC primarily sells mahogany and oak doors since they are typically not commodity doors and demand premium pricing. The doors could be 6 feet 8 inches or 8 feet tall. The doors can also be 36 or 42 inches wide. These doors can have either a glass-top panel or a wood panel. There are five different glasses available for each size of doors. The wood panels can be plain, grooved, with one of three carved designs, plain with a speakeasy window, plain with nailheads, or grooved with nailheads. Finally, all the doors can be shipped unfinished or in one of three colors. This leads to more than a million different combinations that could be sold.

CSC buys the doors as blanks from Asia, South America, and Africa. Thirty-six different companies supply products to CSC. Most of the suppliers also provide the same products to other door manufacturers in the United States. These suppliers have long-term contracts and prices are typically changed every 3 years. Due to the weight and size of the products, they are shipped through ocean containers and freight paid by

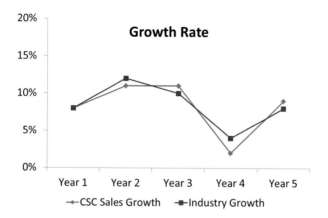

FIGURE 2.2
CSC versus industry growth rate.

suppliers. Sometimes products can be expedited by air freight, but CSC will have to pay for the expedited charge. The minimum order size from suppliers is about four pallets, with each pallet containing 12 door blanks. The minimum order size does not apply for custom door orders.

CSC has experienced average industry growth over the last several years. Figure 2.2 shows the growth rate of the company over the last 5 years. In some years, CSC has grown slightly faster than the market, and slower in other years. But for the most part, CSC has only maintained average growth of the industry. Figure 2.3 shows the earnings before interest and tax (EBIT) as a percent of sales. This shows the profitability level of a company before paying interest to lenders and taxes. Once again, we can see that the profitability of CSC has stalled at 14.7%. It is hard to see any significant improvement in CSC's financials based on the actions taken by CSC.

The shareholders of the company would like to see higher profitability from CSC for their investment. As a result, the shareholders have asked the management team to engage in a full-depth analysis and put a roadmap in place to achieve a 25% EBIT level that is sustainable without additional investment. CSC shareholders want to improve their return on invested capital; hence, the team is expected to improve return on invested capital by at least 5%. The timeline to achieve the results is set at 24 months.

How will the CSC management team achieve these lofty targets for their shareholders? Will CSC add more sales staff to increase sales? Can buying new machines and introducing more automation reduce labor cost? Does outsourcing all production activities provide a competitive edge to CSC?

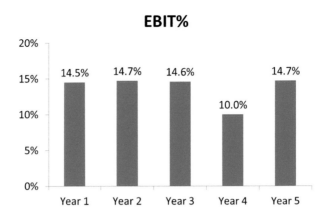

FIGURE 2.3
EBIT margin trend for CSC.

Should CSC start a marketing campaign to drive market penetration into new markets?

To get started, a cross-functional team consisting of employees from all departments is formed by the general manager of CSC, who is the key leader of this transformation. The team is composed of key decision makers and subject matter experts to ensure that decisions are made based on deep knowledge of the business and market. Most of the team members selected for this transformation will be dedicated full time for this initiative since the payback is very high. Only the best talent with credibility in the organization is chosen for the business transformation. But there are some part-time participants in the transformation as well. When selecting part-time participants, clear expectations should be set with the employee and his or her manager in terms of time and deliverables commitment. Part-time participants should view this business transformation project deliverables commitment as either equal to or more important than their current full-time role's responsibilities. A kickoff meeting is scheduled with the team off-site. The purpose of the kickoff meeting is to ensure that everybody understands the current situation and the shareholder expectations. From this starting point, the team is broken into smaller groups as appropriate with a cadence for frequent full-team reviews. The overall progress of this initiative is frequently shared with the shareholders. Regular all-hands review meetings are conducted by the team and all employees of the company. The reviews are both to look back on progress and to look forward to next steps, risks, challenges, and support required for success.

3

Business Performance: Secret Ingredients

In order to improve business performance, we have to understand the purpose of a business to have a common perspective. While there are several explanations for the purpose of a business or corporation, we take a fairly simple approach in this book. We do not cover certain important factors, such as people development, contribution to the society, or environmental impact. These topics are beyond the scope of this book. As mentioned in Chapter 1, the purpose of this book is to develop a comprehensive and well-aligned business transformation plan. For our illustration, based on the expectations from the shareholders, the purpose of a business is to achieve profitable growth with the highest return on capital. There are several books and thought leaders who have discussed the importance of revenue growth and return on invested capital; this book focuses on explaining the "how" rather than the "why" of improving earnings growth and return on invested capital. These two metrics make the biggest impact on a company's value over the long term. Business leaders need to ensure that every action is driving improvement in these two metrics to provide the best results for the shareholders.

Purpose of business = profitable growth with highest return on capital

In order to figure out how we solve for the above purpose of the business, refer back to high school algebra, where we learned that $Y = f(x)$. This means that outcome Y is a function of certain inputs represented as x. Therefore, $Y = f(x1, x2, x3)$ means that outcome Y is a function of inputs $x1$, $x2$, and $x3$.

For example, let us assume that the desired outcome is reduced body weight. The inputs that we could control to reduce body weight include calories consumed, calories exhausted, stress level, and hours of sleep in a day. Notice that we do not take genes into account since that is a factor that we cannot control. You are either born with good genes or not. So it does not make sense to take heredity into account as a factor for improving body weight. Only the inputs that can be controlled or influenced are taken into consideration for achieving the desired outcome.

$$Y = f(x)$$

Body weight

$$= f(\text{calories consumed, calories exhausted, stress level, hours of sleep in a day})$$

Per the above equation, from the right combination of the above x's or factors, we get the desired outcome of weight. Similarly, we can conclude that the purpose of a business is also affected by certain factors that need to be optimized to achieve the desired outcome.

$$Y = f(x)$$

$$\text{Purpose of business} = f(\text{revenue, profitability, capital})$$

So in order to improve the outcome of the business, we will address each factor individually while keeping in mind that they are all interconnected. For example, to increase profits, we cannot simply cut costs by reducing headcount. Taking such a drastic measure could stunt growth. Since the expected outcome for the shareholders of Case Study Company (CSC) is profitable growth and not just growth, we have to keep in mind the interrelationship between the factors. The relationship between the factors is the key reason several companies fail to execute a successful transformation.

Let us further explore each of the factors.

$$\text{Revenue} = \text{Volume} \times \text{Average Selling Price per unit}$$

$$\text{Profit} = \text{Revenue} - \text{Costs} = \text{Revenue} - (\text{Fixed cost} + \text{Variable cost})$$

$$\text{Profit} = (\text{Volume} \times \text{Average Selling Price per unit})$$
$$- \{(\text{Fixed cost per unit} + \text{Variable cost per unit}) \times \text{Volume}\}$$

$$\text{Revenue} = f\left(\text{Volume, Average Selling Price, Product Mix}\right)$$

$$\text{Profit} = f\left(\text{Volume, Average Selling Price, Variable cost, Fixed cost}\right)$$

$$\text{Capital} = f(\text{Revenue, Customer service, Financing rates,}$$
$$\text{Leverage with suppliers, Fixed assets, etc.})$$

The above equations show us that we need to address both the top line of the business and the cost factors that support the business to achieve profitable growth. Also, note that the capital required for a business is a function of revenue growth, customer service, and other factors. Each of the factors is explored further in the following chapters. As you will see, a structured approach is applied to investigate the right drivers of volume, price, and costs to improve the profitability of a company. Randomly making improvements without understanding the interaction could lead to suboptimized outcomes.

The first factor—volume—is addressed by taking the following steps:

1. Identify high-growth market segments.
2. Understand the needs of the high-growth market segments.
3. Understand the current performance to meet the needs of high-growth market segments.
4. Develop an action plan to grow the volume.

Pricing can be improved by a systematic analysis, as shown below:

1. Eliminating unfavorable outliers in pricing
2. Pricing existing products for value
3. New product pricing
4. Improving pricing execution

The process to optimize cost is:

1. Understand the cost drivers.
2. Identify and eliminate noncore costs.
3. Optimize core costs.

The roadmap to right size inventory is:

1. Categorize inventory levels over the year.
2. Segment inventory.
3. Develop an inventory management strategy for each segment.
4. Identify inventory stocking levels.

Finally, in order to improve accounts payable and receivable we use the process below.

1. Improved execution
2. Cycle management
3. Terms rationalization
4. Technology upgrades

The following chapters discuss the application of the above steps at CSC. The specific solution at each company may vary for the problem, but the steps listed above are generic enough to expose the underlying problems. The first step in any business transformation is to identify the root causes of the problem so that the team can then develop solutions to improve the performance of the business. As you will see in the upcoming chapters, by taking a disciplined process of questioning the fundamentals of a business, the team can not only identify the root causes but also develop countermeasures that solve the problem permanently.

4

Revenue Growth: The Elusive Unicorn

In this chapter, we discuss how Case Study Company's (CSC) management team approaches revenue growth. For any company, the top-line revenue growth trend indicates the value of the business in the market. A company that is surviving without good revenue growth is just dying a slow death. Companies that generate more profits solely by cost-cutting actions or financial engineering cannot survive in the long term. It is a flawed business model. CSC business leaders are keeping in mind that their management charge is to achieve *profitable growth* and not just growing sales without higher margin. This requires a good understanding of all the drivers of revenue and making the right improvements for each lever.

$$\text{Revenue} = f\left(\text{Volume, Average Selling Price per unit, Product Mix}\right)$$

There are two primary ways to grow a business—organic growth and inorganic growth. Organic growth is a result of selling more of existing products or services to existing customers or new customers, product expansion, licensing, and so forth. Inorganic growth is a result of mergers and acquisitions. Both approaches have their advantages and disadvantages, as shown in Table 4.1. For the discussion of this book, we stick to organic growth factors only.

So where will the CSC team look for revenue growth?

- Will they just increase the price across all the product lines and gain revenue?
- Will the customers buy at the higher price point?
- Can CSC sell more by providing promotions to the customers?
- Should CSC introduce new products to the market?

TABLE 4.1

Organic versus Inorganic Growth Strategies

Growth strategy	Pros	Cons
Organic	Lower up-front investment	Lower growth rate
	Limited risk exposure	Lower results certainty
Inorganic	Faster growth rate	Higher up-front cost
	Proven results	Integration risk

In order to answer these questions, the CSC team will take a holistic view of the business from a market perspective as well as their product portfolio. Ensuring that the right products and value are provided to the right segments of the market is the challenge for CSC. A data-driven market and product portfolio performance analysis will solve the challenge.

There are various schools of thought on how market segmentation should be conducted. Some marketing experts recommend segmenting the market based on the needs of the segment, while others propose segmenting the market based on the characteristics of the segment, and still others advocate for segmenting the market based on customer profiles that are a combination of the other two methods of segmentation. Our experience has been to take an approach that makes sense and is actionable, as opposed to arguing on theoretical validity.

First, the team looks at the growth, profitability, and market share characteristics of the four market segments. Figure 4.1 shows the compounded annual growth rate (CAGR), earnings before interest and tax (EBIT) percentage, market size, and market share of each market segment. The four market segments are:

1. Custom doors—These are completely custom doors where the customer selects the design, wood, glass, and so forth. These are generally high-end doors used for expensive homes. The customer requests are typically taken by the sales team, and the engineering team in CSC develops the drawings and specifications for the suppliers. Once the suppliers build the doors, they are shipped to CSC. CSC then processes these doors and ships them to the customer. These doors are generally ordered as one lot, processed as one lot, and shipped as one lot since they are usually needed for one particular home or group of homes.

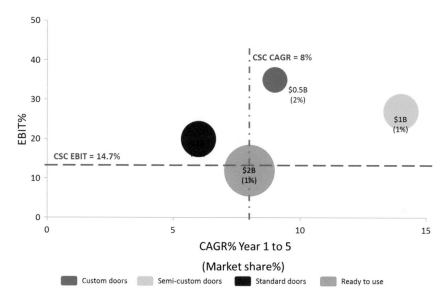

FIGURE 4.1
Market segment CAGR, EBIT, market size, and market share.

2. Semicustom doors—These doors are shown in the product catalog, but they can be slightly customized by the customer. For example, the customer can choose to have only two grooves in the bottom panel instead of the standard four grooves, or the customer may choose to have the door blanks sold by CSC with a custom glass specified by the customer.

3. Standard doors—These are doors that CSC sells to the customers without any changes, for example, the Sierra product line—oak doors that have a glass in the top panel with an inlay of a mountain range in wrought iron. These doors are available in heights of 8 feet and 6 feet 8 inches. The doors are always the standard width of 3 feet. No customization is available for these doors.

4. Ready to use—These are doors sold with hardware (lock set, hinges, etc.), primarily to big-box stores and wholesalers.

The x-axis shows the CAGR for each market segment. Similarly, the y-axis shows the EBIT margin for each of the market segments based on CSC's products in the segment. The size of the bubble is the North American market size, and in parentheses the CSC market share for the segment is shown. For example, the custom door market segment is growing at 9%, with an EBIT of 35%; the market size is $0.5 billion in

North America; and the CSC market share is 2%. The dash lines represent the average EBIT margin percentage and the average CAGR of CSC.

The CSC management team believes that the growth and profitability trends over the last 5 years will continue into the future. The chart also shows how the market segments are performing with respect to CSC's overall EBIT margin and growth rate. The following are the key takeaways for the team from the above analysis:

- Increase market share in custom doors and semicustom door market segment
- In the ready-to-use doors segment, which has an average growth rate, we have to increase margin.
- Limit or eliminate the presence in standard doors.

With this high-level view of the market, CSC wants to dig a level deeper. To further understand the performance of CSC's current product offerings, the team charts the product lines as shown in Figure 4.2 with respect to CAGR and EBIT margin. The product lines are represented as dots in the market segments' respective colors. The chart is divided into four zones based on their relative CAGR and EBIT levels. The company overall CAGR and EBIT percentage are also shown.

From Revenue

$$= f\left(\text{Volume, Average Selling Price, Mix}\right); \text{ we will first explore volume.}$$

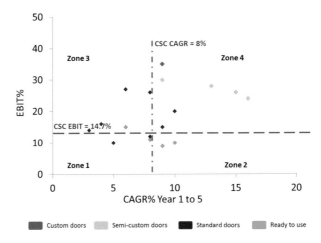

FIGURE 4.2
Product line CAGR versus EBIT margin.

VOLUME

The first factor to improve the revenue is volume. Volume is measured as the number of units sold. In the case of CSC, it is the number of doors sold to their customers. We will discuss the approach to organic growth in the business, which does not include growth through acquisitions. However, the roadmap shown below can be used as a screen to evaluate acquisition target companies on their potential for volume growth.

Driving volume growth has several benefits to a business. Some of the benefits are:

- Company revenue increases
- More of the fixed costs of the business gets absorbed with higher volume
- Increased market share, which could lead to pricing power and other benefits
- Increased confidence in the business model by all the stakeholders of the company

How can CSC increase the volume of sales? Should they add more salespeople? Will CSC benefit from dropping the price of the doors? Does a marketing campaign generate more revenue? Will increasing product portfolio drive more volume to the business?

In order to answer the above questions and drive volume into the business, the CSC team takes a disciplined approach. CSC approaches volume growth by taking the steps below.

1. Identify high-growth market segments.
2. Understand the needs of the high-growth market segments.
3. Understand the current performance to meet the needs of the high-growth market segments.
4. Develop an action plan to grow the volume.

1. Identify High-Growth Market Segments

For a company to grow, it should participate primarily in the growing segments of the market. Trying to grow at an above-market pace by participating in low-growth segments is like flying against headwinds; this creates a lot of friction and little progress. Clearly segmenting the market into suitable categories and focusing on the growth segments provides a better growth trajectory.

In order to drive volume, CSC has to participate in the high-growth market segments from Figure 4.2. Table 4.2 shows the comparative segment and product line growth. A market segment has red shading in the market CAGR column because the CAGR for the market segment is lower than CSC's CAGR of 8%. In other words, these market segments have below-average CAGR performance compared with CSC. However, market segments that have CAGR performance that is equal to or greater than CSC's average of 8% are shaded green. So in order for CSC to grow volume, they should participate primarily in the green-shaded market segments.

Below are some takeaways from this analysis:

- If both the market segment and product line CAGRs are red, the performance column is red. This means that the CSC team chooses to rationalize this product line from their offering.

TABLE 4.2

Market Segment versus Product Line CAGR

Market Segment	Market CAGR	Product Line	Product Line CAGR	Performance
Custom	9%	Custom doors	7%	
Semicustom	14%	PL C1	9%	
Semicustom	14%	PL C2	16%	
Semicustom	14%	PL C3	13%	
Semicustom	14%	PL C4	15%	
Standard	6%	PL S1	3%	
Standard	6%	PL S2	10%	
Standard	6%	PL S3	8%	
Standard	6%	PL S4	5%	
Standard	6%	PL S5	8%	
Standard	6%	PL S6	9%	
Standard	6%	PL S7	4%	
Standard	6%	PL S8	6%	
Ready to use	8%	PL R1	6%	
Ready to use	8%	PL R2	9%	
Ready to use	8%	PL R3	10%	
Ready to use	8%	PL R4	8%	

- If either the market segment or product line CAGR is red, the performance column is yellow. This means that the CSC team needs to investigate further.
- If both the market segment and product line CAGRs are green, the performance column is green. This means that the CSC team will keep the product line and figure out how to get more growth from it.

2. Understand the Needs of the High-Growth Market Segments

After identifying the faster-growing segments, companies need to understand the various factors that drive growth in these segments. In other words, the consumers in the faster-growing segments have certain needs, and these needs could be product or service related. To win in the fast-growing market segments, companies should understand the needs of the customers through various sources.

Since above-average growth can be achieved from the custom and semicustom door segments, CSC decides to conduct a voice of the customer (VOC) study in order to grow in these segments. In the construction industry, there are several players in the value chain—manufacturers, distributors, wholesalers, builders, and so forth. From experience, the CSC team knows that the key decision makers for selecting the doors for a construction project are the builders in the value chain. Once the builders accept the door manufacturer, they pass on that information to their distributor. Though the distributor is the direct customer that the door manufacturers have to ship product to and negotiate pricing with, the voice of the builder is the most valuable in the value chain. The builders are the key decision makers of the door manufacturer based on the product and service profile of the door manufacturer. Hence, for conducting VOC study the team at CSC will focus on the builders across North America.

To conduct the VOC study, the CSC team decides to use a web service since they already have the email addresses for all their customers and potential customers. A brief VOC survey is set up with the following questions:

1. Are you a current customer of CSC?
2. Have you done business with CSC before?
3. What are your deciding factors in selecting a door manufacturer?
4. List your top three decision-making factors to select a door manufacturer.

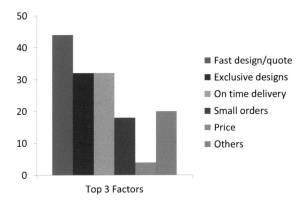

FIGURE 4.3
Top three factors for deciding custom door manufacturer.

5. If a current customer or you have done business with CSC before, how would you rate CSC's performance? (Select from drop-down list: best of all door manufacturers, average of all door manufacturers, and below other door manufacturers.)
6. Other comments to serve you better (free text box).

Two separate studies were conducted for custom door and semicustom door market segments. Emails were sent to key decision makers in these companies. The results from the VOC study are shown below.

Figure 4.3 shows the top three factors that affect the buying decision for the custom door market segment. The sample size is 47 builders nationally. Based on the VOC study, the top three factors for choosing a custom door manufacturer are:

1. Fast design/quote process
2. Exclusive designs
3. On-time delivery of order

Figure 4.4 shows the top three factors that affect the buying decision for the semicustom door market segment. The sample size is 70 builders nationally. Based on the VOC study, the top three factors for choosing a semicustom door manufacturer are:

- More customization options
- Ease of business
- Lead time

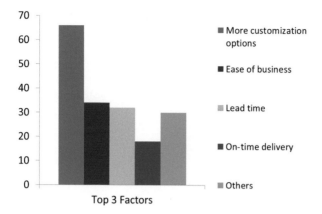

FIGURE 4.4
Top three factors for deciding semicustom door manufacturer.

3. Understand the Current Performance to Meet the Needs of the High-Growth Market Segments

Apart from understanding the needs of the customers, CSC also needs to know where they stand with respect to customer needs. Hence, the VOC survey was designed to make sure that CSC gets feedback on their current performance level. Based on the feedback, CSC can prioritize their focus for improvements and investments in the business.

In the VOC study, question 5 was, how would the customers rate CSC's performance with respect to the top three important factors in the custom door segment? The summary of this survey is shown in Figure 4.5.

From this survey, CSC also learns that about half the customers think their performance is average as compared to their competitors. About 22% of the customers think CSC's performance is below average. In order to grow in the custom door market, CSC needs to improve their speed to design, provide exclusive designs, and improve on-time delivery of orders.

In the VOC study, question 5 was, how would the customers rate CSC's performance with respect to the top three important factors in the semicustom door segment? The summary of this survey is shown in Figure 4.6.

From this survey, CSC also learns that about 66% of the customers think their performance is below that of their competitors. In order to grow in the semicustom door market, CSC needs to provide more customization options, reduce order lead time, and improve on-time delivery.

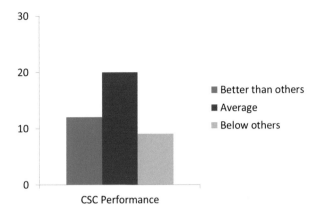

FIGURE 4.5
Performance feedback for custom door market.

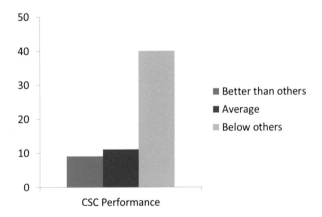

FIGURE 4.6
Performance feedback for semicustom door market.

4. Develop an Action Plan to Grow the Volume

In summary, to drive volume growth CSC needs to do the following:

- Custom door market segment:
  - Implement a faster design/quote process
  - Provide more exclusive designs
  - Improve on-time delivery
- Semicustom door market segment:
  - Provide more customization options
  - Improve the ease of conducting business with CSC
  - Reduce lead time

- Investigate the standard door market segment since growth is below average and low margin. CSC cannot immediately drop the standard doors product lines since this will lead to a drop in revenue for the short term.

The method for achieving the above goals is discussed in the cost optimization section, where all the operational changes are addressed. One of the key actions that the CSC team takes is to align and provide more customization options for certain builders that are growing faster than the market. For example, a builder in Colorado is growing at about 15% year over year. This builder is building homes at about a $700,000 price range on hilly surfaces to provide an upscale and modern look. So CSC provides more customization options to this builder to select various features to create an upscale and modern look.

Based on the various actions from the CSC team, Table 4.3 shows how CSC can increase market share and CAGR over the next 5 years. CSC assumes that they will maintain the current growth rate for the standard door and ready-to-use door market segments. The custom door product line has to grow at a compounded rate of 25% to double the market share since the market itself is growing at 9% and the current growth rate is 7%. Similarly, the semicustom door product line has to grow 31% year over year to double market share since the market itself is growing at 14% and the current growth rate is 14%. At the bottom of Table 4.3, we see that the overall company sales are $115 million in 5 years, which represents a compounded growth rate of 14%.

TABLE 4.3

CSC Sales Growth Summary

		Current	**In 5 Years**
Custom	Market share	2%	4%
	CAGR	7%	2.5%
	Custom door sales	$10M	$30.5M
Semicustom	Market share	1%	2%
	CAGR	14%	31%
	Semicustom door sales	$10M	$38.5M
CSC	Market share	2%	3%
	CAGR	8%	14%
	Total sales	$60M	$115M

As shown above, volume growth can be achieved by taking a systematic approach of:

1. Identify high-growth market segments.
2. Understand the needs of the high-growth market segments.
3. Understand the current performance to meet the needs of the high-growth market segments.
4. Develop an action plan to grow the volume.

PRICING

In order to increase revenue, increasing the average selling price (ASP) has an immediate effect. Pricing is usually the fastest and most successful lever to improve revenue and profitability. Pricing also creates a brand perception and image of value to customers. Hence, price setting should be carefully considered not just by the marketing team, but also by the senior leaders of the business to understand the impact created by price in the market. There are several ways to increase ASP:

1. Eliminating unfavorable outliers in pricing
2. Pricing existing products for value
3. New product pricing
4. Improving pricing execution

1. Eliminating Unfavorable Outliers

A fast way to improve ASP would be to find outliers and correct them. Outliers could be products, customers, industries, or segments that are not priced appropriately. Generally, we find several customers who are priced below average and have a low volume of business. These could be fixed fairly easily with some fundamental analysis of factors used for providing pricing to customers.

First, the CSC team starts their pricing study by looking at how they have priced their products with respect to their customers' volume. Since the custom doors are unique offerings, each time that they are offered the CSC team investigates the pricing for this market separately. Figure 4.7 shows the ASP and annual sales volume by customer and part number combination.

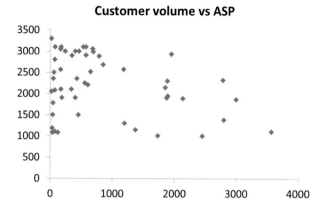

FIGURE 4.7
Annual volume versus ASP by customer.

The CSC team realizes that customers in zone 1 from Figure 4.7 are priced below the median price of $2300 and under the median annual volume of 1000 doors. For lower-volume customers, you would expect to have higher prices, but these customers were not priced as expected. So the CSC team investigates further to understand the reasons for lower prices to these customers. Upon investigation, the reasons they find are as follows:

1. Customers missed expected volume—The sales team provides a price based on the expected volume from the customer throughout the year, but these customers miss their volume.
2. Customers have a high margin though the price is low—no action for this.
3. CSC sales provided a lower price to penetrate into a new region, but never went back and increased prices to normal.
4. Multiple discounts were applied by customers to lower the price.

The CSC team also looks at the price spread by product line to figure out if there are gaps. Figure 4.8 shows the pricing spread by product line for standard doors and ready-to-use doors. This chart shows that the exact same product was sold at different prices to different customers, which is acceptable. However, for product lines with a very high spread, like S2, S3, S7, and R1, the CSC team decides to investigate further. On further analysis, the team realizes that the reasons for wide spreads are:

• Improper price setting with multiple discounts.
• The expected volume from customers was not realized.

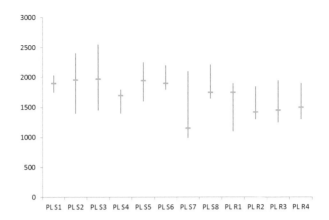

FIGURE 4.8
Pricing spread by product line.

2. Pricing Existing Products for Value

The pricing for a product or service has to be a strategy to exert maximum value for the product or service offered to the target customer. Unfortunately, most companies do not have a good pricing strategy and pricing is usually a series of discrete opinions and decisions. It is very common to see companies use cost-plus pricing or rely on the opinions of the sales force to set pricing and then try to justify their reason for this type of pricing. Worse, some companies bring up the example of a price increase that was passed to a customer (without any logical value analysis) in the past and the loss of business as a result of that action. A couple of these examples are enough to justify to the business managers that "we are different."

The value of a product or service is influenced by various factors, such as economic, emotional, social, and other benefits to the buyer. By focusing on value-based pricing, companies can achieve the optimal price for the product and constantly strive for value creation in the company for the customers. By understanding the value of product features to the customers, companies can create better customer segmentation based on customer needs and develop more targeted products with the right pricing to win in the market.

Since the growth of CSC is dependent on custom and semicustom doors, CSC will focus their efforts on these two product lines. The custom door and semicustom door product lines are different almost every time, so the pricing of these product lines is critical. In the past, the marketing team at CSC would follow a cost-plus approach to price the custom doors and semicustom doors. The CSC marketing team would obtain the cost of production of a door from finance and add other overheads and a suitable profit to arrive at the price of the door for the customer. There was no discussion of value to the customer and how CSC can price the product based on value. This leads to potential profits missed due to lack of understanding what the customer is really willing to pay for the product. When we price for value, we can not only improve profitability but also improve brand image and avoid commoditizing the product in the market.

Below is a cost-plus approach used in CSC. If a customer for a semicustom door requested an 8-foot mahogany door with special glass and four grooves in the bottom panel, the pricing logic would be as shown below.

Door blank	$800
Glass insert	$300
Production cost	$200
Other cost	$150
Total cost	$1450
Expected profit (40%)	$580
Price of door	$2030

For the same customer, if the CSC team understands the value of providing some customization, they can price the product higher. As shown below, CSC can start with the pricing of a comparable product offering and add in the value of customization. The value of an impressive entryway to a home worth more than half-million dollars can be estimated by industry experience, interviewing customers, conducting tests, and so forth. The new logic for pricing for value would be as shown below.

Comparable product offering	$2000
Value of sourcing specific glass	$200
Value of an impressive entryway to $500K+ home	$500
Price of door	$2700

As you can see, the same product could be priced about 30% higher. This increase in price directly impacts the bottom line of the company. The CSC team agrees that the new logic makes sense because based on their experience, they have priced the exact same customization to different customers at different prices. So the product discussed above as an example was sold to customers at different price points and, in some cases, to the same customer at different prices. In reality, the actual price is somewhere between current cost plus and the full value of the product to the customer.

So in order to improve pricing for current and new products, CSC decides to use a value-based pricing model. The team is confident that they can increase their ASP by 10% by applying the principle of value-based pricing.

3. New Products Pricing

As new products and services are introduced, companies have a golden opportunity to create a strong position in the market and maximize the value captured in earnings. It is very important for companies to understand the value of the products being introduced, so the marketing and advertising efforts can be more focused toward the target customers. Once again, it is important to align the new product strategy with the corporate strategy—maximize market share, high profitability, average industry growth, and so forth, so that the pricing of the new product will enable the achievement of the corporate strategy.

When new products are introduced, the CSC team decides to price the new products based on value to the customer. Strategically, the goal for the CSC marketing team is to ensure that as new products are introduced, the median ASP in Figure 4.7 is constantly increasing. So even if the volume is flat, the revenue is still growing. The marketing team can achieve higher prices by introducing more value-added features to customers, such as customization options, customer inventory management, better lead times, and product reliability. The actions taken in step 2 above to determine value will be used to set the price of new products as opposed to a cost-plus model. Introducing new products into the market at the right price level for the right market subsegments ensures a higher win rate. A higher win rate in turn leads to higher volumes and sales efficiency.

4. Improving Pricing Execution

The above steps discuss how to set the price; this step is about how to get the price. Pricing execution is about ensuring that the expected or budgeted price is realized in the financial statements. In other words, during the budgeting process finance makes certain assumptions on price, whether or not the realized price meets the budgeted price; this is a measure of pricing execution. There are several factors that affect pricing execution—pricing practices, discounts/promotions, special rebates, manual overwrites, payment terms, new market entry, and so forth. It is important to remember that poor pricing execution is not because of untalented people; poor pricing execution is because of poor processes, policies, procedures, and organization alignment. Solutions to improve pricing execution should be focused on these factors to prevent profit leaks. In some industries, poor pricing execution could lead to compliance issues and cause business continuity risk.

CSC started the pricing execution analysis from the product line level. Figure 4.9 shows the expected price and the actual price by product line. Custom doors were not included because by nature they are custom and price varies by the features. As highlighted, product lines R1, R3, and S7 have the largest gaps between their budgeted and actual price.

CSC wants to further understand the factors that affect pricing execution. Figure 4.10 shows a waterfall chart that represents the various factors that lead to a difference between budgeted price and actual price. CSC gathers this data by comparing the actual invoice price to the price list or budgeted price for each door. The gap between the median price of $2300 and budgeted price of $2600 is due to the factors shown in Figure 4.10. Discounts are price reductions provided for a seasonal promotion, to attract a customer, or

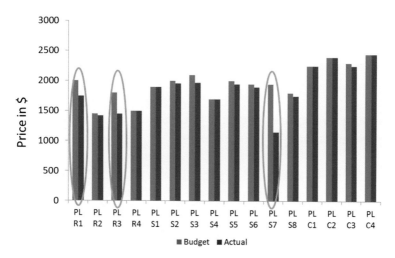

FIGURE 4.9
Budgeted versus actual price by product line.

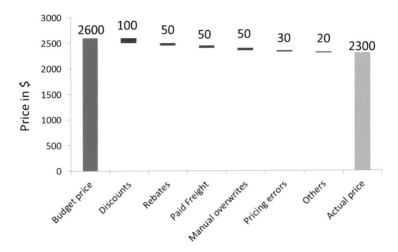

FIGURE 4.10
Factors that cause a drop from the budgeted price to the actual price.

to enter a new region for sales expansion. Rebates are generally provided based on some volume commitment that the customers meet. It is important to note that rebates and discounts or promotions are different. "Paid freight" is the expedited freight paid by CSC to customers for missing delivery commitment. "Manual overwrites" are changes made to the price of a product based on the directions of either the sales team or senior leadership. Pricing errors are caused due to typos or miscalculating costs or price.

___

SUMMARY

In summary, to improve pricing the CSC marketing team is provided with the following actions:

1. Implement value-based pricing. In the past, CSC usually applied a cost-plus approach to price their products in the market. Going forward, CSC will figure out value to the customer based on market segment, value of homes being built, level of customization, region, and so forth. By implementing a value-based pricing strategy, CSC is confident that they can increase their ASP by 10% for custom doors, semicustom doors, and ready-to-use doors.

2. Improve the contract management process. When customers are provided a certain price based on an expected volume, the marketing team will ensure that the contract with the customer mentions minimum quantity and tiered pricing. Additionally, there will be a periodic contract review process to ensure that all customers are meeting the expected volume. By improving the contract management process, CSC is confident that they can improve their ASP by about 2.4% for half the customers buying semicustom doors, standard doors, and ready-to-use doors.

3. Review pricing strategy for new region penetration. Historically, the CSC marketing team would price the products lower to penetrate a new region, but they would never go back and adjust the pricing unless someone from finance complained. This strategy of pricing low would usually affect the brand image as well. So CSC decided to price based on value and sell at normal prices. The CSC team also determined that the strategy of dropping price to enter a new market should be stopped, and they should employ selling based on their core competency of customization and good customer service. By improving the pricing strategy for new regions, CSC is confident that they can improve their ASP by 1.1%.

4. Improve management of discounts and promotions. Historically, promotions were offered by CSC, but individual salesmen also offered some discounts to customers. This resulted in reducing the price of the product and drove the wrong behaviors. Going forward, CSC decided that all discounts and promotions will only be offered by the marketing managers, which will prevent the bundling of discounts. A discount/promotion approval hierarchy is established. Based on this change, CSC is confident that they can improve their ASP by 1%.

5. Improve pricing policy to eliminate manual overwrites. These changes to the price were made by the sales team or senior leaders based on commitments they were making to the customers outside of the price list or policy. This was a result of poor enforcement of pricing policies. By eliminating manual overwrites, the CSC team is confident that they can improve their ASP by 0.5%.

6. Mistake-proof the order entry process. CSC realizes that there were typos and miscommunication issues that were leading to lower ASP and profit. By implementing a mistake-proof process to enter price, the CSC team is confident that they can improve their ASP by 0.2%.

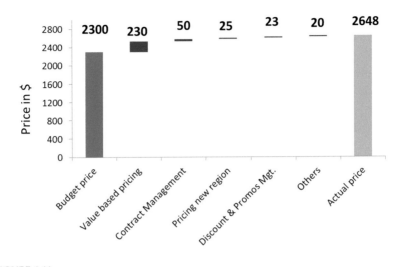

FIGURE 4.11
Actions from pricing to increase ASP.

Figure 4.11 shows how the various actions of the CSC team for pricing can increase the ASP. CSC selling doors at an ASP of $2648 is an increase of about 15% from the current ASP of $2300. These changes have to be supported and enforced from top leadership to achieve and sustain the results.

As shown above, ASP can be increased by:

1. Eliminating unfavorable outliers in pricing
2. Pricing existing products for value
3. New product pricing
4. Improving pricing execution

PRODUCT MIX

The last factor to grow revenue is to improve the product mix. By "product mix," we refer to the content of higher-margin products in sales as opposed to lower-margin products. For example, let us consider a company that sells two products, A and B; A has a higher margin and B has a lower margin. One way to grow revenue and/or profitability is to increase the sales of product A, though total units sold may be the same. By selling more of product B, the company will be growing, but with weaker profitability.

Companies need to ensure they have a strong pipeline of products or services under development to constantly improve the product mix.

For CSC, the higher-margin product lines are in custom doors and semicustom doors, as shown in Figure 4.1. Hence, to improve the mix, the CSC team focuses on selling more custom and semicustom doors as opposed to standard and ready-to-use doors. From earlier discussion on growing volume, CSC has prioritized growing the custom and semicustom doors as the key driver of their growth strategy. Since the EBIT percentages for custom and semicustom doors are higher, as CSC sells more doors in these two market segments, the mix becomes favorable to growing CSC's profitability.

From Table 4.2, the product lines with a red performance rating are eliminated and substituted by similar product lines with a green rating. For example, PL S4 is similar to PL S5, so the CSC sales team is trained to promote PL S5 instead of PL S4 when customers seek out PL S4. Of course, the strongest push back will be from the sales team, since they will have certain customers who buy several other door product lines along with the unfavorable product lines. The approach that the CSC team should take to avoid losing customers is as follows:

- First, replace red performance rating products with existing products that have a green performance rating from Table 4.2.
- Second, increase the price for lower-margin products.
- Third, treat the red performance rating products as custom doors. This means that the customers should order a larger size at a higher price and the product will be shipped direct from supplier to customer.

Figure 4.12 shows how revenue will grow over the next 5 years at CSC based on the actions from volume growth, pricing, and product mix improvement. This represents an annual CAGR of 17.2%; this is more than twice the current CAGR of 8%!

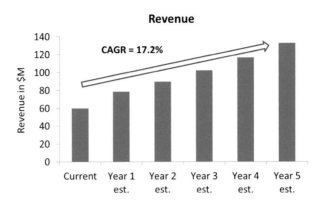

FIGURE 4.12
Actions from volume and pricing analysis to increase revenue.

Practical Tips

- Most industry/trade magazines can provide market share, growth rate, and competitor information for a much lower price than consultants.
- Market data does not have to be exact. For example, whether the market size of a product line is 17 million or 16 million is not as important as the approximate value.
- If the market data trend is available for 3 years, that is useful in identifying any shifts in customer preference or macroeconomic factors.
- Sometimes segmentation by microsegments may be necessary to identify specific needs of the customers. For example, in the automobile market, the needs of a millennial urban female (compact, swift, easy parking, eco-friendly) are much different than the needs of a middle-aged suburban-dwelling female (space for kids and their friends, crash safety, cup holders, and trays).
- If the EBIT percentage is not clearly available for your product lines, then use the gross profit percentage for the product lines as long as there are not huge swings to SG&A (selling, general, administrative) costs between the product lines.
- To grow sales, sometimes conducting a heat map of territory coverage by sales representative may help you identify opportunities.
- To conduct the VOC study, certain temporary placement agencies have experienced contractors that can be used to call the customers or send emails and ensure follow-through on the process.

- College interns could also be used to conduct VOC studies.
- Do not use only your sales team for the VOC study. Sometimes this feedback could be the sales team's own opinions.
- Offering an incentive for respondents of the VOC study can improve its success rate.
- Sometimes VOC studies may be needed from several participants in a value chain before making any changes.
- There are other actions that can be taken to improve the mix, such as higher sales incentive for sales reps to sell custom and semicustom doors, limiting the sales volume of lower-margin doors, introducing more models of semicustom doors, and acquiring businesses with higher profitability.
- If products are technology driven, understanding the current product portfolio by technology for the market needs may reveal gaps.
- Sometimes customers of the same volume and product may be charged different prices due to varied value-added services provided. The value-added services vary by industry. Make sure you chart the value-added services as a bubble chart to reflect the same.
- Market and competitor analysis are key ingredients for price setting. The data can be achieved by third-party reports, field intelligence, or surveys.
- An important factor while addressing pricing is the supply and demand balance in the market. If there is sufficient supply of a similar product or service in the market, that becomes a factor to consider while setting price since customers can always switch to the alternate supply. If a market is oversupplied, a tactic that can be deployed is to provide more intangible services, such as faster lead time, inventory management, payment terms, and co-branding, to create barriers for switching.
- Value-based pricing can be achieved only if sales leaders are selling value to customers and not just volume discounts.
- Companies with assets that may lose revenue forever if not utilized to produce value should consider the revenue management tactics deployed by airlines and hospitality industries.

5

Cost Optimization: Crack the Nut without Creating a Mess

Unfortunately, many companies are disconnected in their top-line growth plan and their cost improvement plan. While the marketing department in a company is trying to win business by providing better service, the finance department may be cutting the travel budget, assuming that travel to customer sites is an unneeded cost. Also, the procurement department may be negotiating a lower cost with a freight carrier who will only transport full truckloads, which leads to the delivery of parts to customers only on a certain day of the week. Hence, it is very important to understand the following about building a sustainable business: *The growth strategy should be based on customer needs. The operations strategy should be to support the growth strategy with the optimum cost structure and competencies in the business. The finance strategy should be to ensure that the business is appropriately funded to achieve the growth plan through the competencies required.*

Cost optimization can provide several benefits to a business:

- Increased profitability
- Flexibility to pass on price reductions to customers to either gain or retain business
- Higher returns to shareholders
- Simplification of processes
- Clear roles and responsibilities
- Engaged workforce

When companies aim for cost optimization, all employees can get engaged in constantly thinking about ways to improve the business operations. Not all employees in a company can be engaged in driving sales, since not all employees make contact with customers. However, all employees affect the cost of operating a business, so engaging all employees in cost optimization through various programs such as Lean manufacturing, Six Sigma, and total quality control can create an engaged workforce and profitability for the company. For these programs to be successful, a very deep understanding of engagement and commitment is required from the senior leadership of the organization.

After understanding how CSC can grow the top line for the business, the team focuses on the bottom line. CSC has to make sure that while the business is growing, their profitability is growing as well. More importantly, CSC should have the core processes and capabilities required to achieve the top-line growth plan laid out by the team. It is very important to understand that CSC's focus is not just cost reduction but also cost optimization. Cost reduction can be achieved for several years by cutting staff, offshoring, outsourcing, reducing investment, and so forth. But this method of cost reduction, without a focus on the actions required to build a sustainable business, will lead to failure. So CSC follows a methodical process to understand and optimize the costs of the business.

In CSC, the team takes a methodical process to understand and optimize the costs of the business as shown below.

1. Understand the cost drivers.
2. Identify and eliminate noncore costs.
3. Optimize core costs.

1. UNDERSTAND THE COST DRIVERS

In order to understand the cost elements of a company, we should start with the company's income statement. There are several different ways to dissect the income statement—fixed, variable, direct, indirect, and so forth. But a practical way to break down the costs would be such that it is easy to understand what is driving the costs and what is actionable to make changes. Also, we should look at the costs over a period to see if there is a significant shift in any category.

CSC reviews their income statements for the last 3 years and the current year, as shown in Table 5.1. CSC breaks cost down by categories so that the team members can take action. For example, direct material cost is called

TABLE 5.1

Income Statement for CSC

	3 Years Ago	2 Years Ago	1 Year Ago	Current
Sales	$48,618,505	$53,966,541	$55,045,872	$60,000,000
Direct material	$19,447,402	$23,205,613	$23,119,266	$25,800,000
Direct labor	$5,850,000	$5,940,000	$6,180,000	$6,000,000
Indirect material	$1,944,740	$1,618,996	$2,201,835	$1,800,000
Indirect labor	$3,700,000	$3,777,658	$4,600,000	$4,200,000
Lease		$240,300	$840,000	$840,000
Freight	$210,000	$454,859	$550,184	$600,000
Other manufacturing expenses	$400,000	$400,000	$500,000	$600,000
Depreciation	$6,000,000	$6,000,000	$6,000,000	$6,000,000
Gross profit	**$11,066,363**	**$12,329,115**	**$11,054,587**	**$14,160,000**
SG&A	$3,800,000	$4,050,000	$5,000,000	$4,840,000
Other expenses	$119,443	$400,000	$550,000	$500,000
EBIT	**$7,146,920**	**$7,879,115**	**$5,504,587**	**$8,820,000**

out since the CSC team can brainstorm how they can improve their spend on direct materials and assign the procurement team to take actions.

Sales represents the total revenue of the company. Direct material is the total spend in the year for purchasing door blanks, glass inserts, door locksets, and door stains. Direct labor is the total spend on salaries, overtime, and benefits for production workers. These workers are paid on an hourly rate and their labor is assigned to each production order. Indirect material is the spend on sanding paper, glue, nails, electricity, and so forth. Indirect labor is the salaries and benefits paid for production and supply chain management, material handlers, and warehouse employees. Lease was a new cost incurred by CSC for their warehouse on West Coast 2 years ago. Since the factory is owned by CSC, there is no lease expense. Freight is the cost of freight incurred by CSC to ship to customers and the warehouse on the West Coast. Other manufacturing expenses are captured in a miscellaneous category. SG&A (selling, general, administrative) encompasses the salaries and benefits of management, engineering, the sales team, and marketing, as well as selling expenses. Other expenses include one-off expenses the company incurs, such as legal fees, consulting fees, and one-time payments.

By merely looking at the absolute value of a cost category, it will be hard to make any inferences. Hence, the CSC team decides to normalize the costs to a percentage of sales. This should show if the costs in any of the categories are increasing, decreasing, or staying flat as a percentage

TABLE 5.2

Income Statement for CSC as Percentage of Sales

	3 Years Ago	2 Years Ago	1 Year Ago	Current
Sales	100%	100%	100%	100%
Direct material	40.0%	43.0%	42.0%	43.0%
Direct labor	12.0%	11.0%	11.2%	10.0%
Indirect material	4.0%	3.0%	4.0%	3.0%
Indirect labor	7.6%	7.0%	8.4%	7.0%
Lease	0.0%	0.4%	1.5%	1.4%
Freight	0.4%	0.8%	1.0%	1.0%
Other manufacturing expenses	0.8%	0.7%	0.9%	1.0%
Depreciation	12.3%	11.1%	10.9%	10.0%
Gross profit	**22.8%**	**22.8%**	**20.1%**	**23.6%**
SG&A	7.8%	7.5%	9.1%	8.1%
Other expenses	0.2%	0.7%	1.0%	0.8%
EBIT	**14.7%**	**14.6%**	**10.0%**	**14.7%**

of sales, which impacts the profit margin for CSC. Table 5.2 shows the same income statement with the cost categories as a percentage of sales. We can quickly see that direct material is the largest portion of the total cost, about 43%. The second largest contributor to cost is direct labor, though CSC has made some improvement over the last year. Lease, which is a new cost category for CSC, is about 1.5% of sales. The warehouse setup on the West Coast was primarily to increase the sales of the standard door market segment by being able to ship sooner to distributors on the West Coast. The freight cost has gone up from 0.4% of sales to 1% of sales, primarily due to the West Coast warehouse. The cost of shipping doors from the factory to the West Coast warehouse has to be picked up by CSC. The depreciation of assets as a percentage of sales has improved primarily due to more volume being processed with the same level of investment in assets.

Below are some quick observations based on the trend of the normalized cost data.

- High cost drivers—Direct material and direct labor make up more than 50% of sales.
- New cost drivers—Lease of the new warehouse on West Coast.
- Wrong cost trend—Freight cost has increased primarily due to shipment to the West Coast warehouse.
- Improved cost trend—Direct labor and gross profit.

2. IDENTIFY AND ELIMINATE NONCORE COSTS

In order to complete this step, we need to understand the definition of noncore costs. Different books provide different definitions for core and noncore cost. For our common grounding, we use the following definition. Noncore cost is any cost that is incurred by the business that does not support the growth strategy of the business and/or cost incurred by the business that does not provide a competitive advantage in the marketplace. This definition applies for all activities that the company performs. We may not be able to solve all noncore costs at once, but over time the business should aim for eliminating these costs since they drag down the performance of the business.

One easy subcategory of noncore cost is cost of poor quality. This is the cost that a business incurs due to scrap, rework, reprocessing, warranty claims, and so forth. Different companies have different definitions for the cost of poor quality. As you can imagine, the cost of poor quality leads to material waste, direct labor waste, unnecessary management time, expediting orders, excess inventory, inconsistent lead times, poor customer delivery, and so forth. Some costs may not be easily captured in an income statement, for example, the impact of inconsistent lead time. However, any business transformation should take a hard look at the cost of poor quality and its impact not only on cost, but also on customer satisfaction, which could affect sales and the growth strategy of a company. For simplicity purposes, we will not show any cost of poor quality at CSC, but in reality, this could be more than 10% of sales in some companies. The objective should be to ensure that the cost of poor quality is eliminated or significantly reduced.

At CSC, to identify the noncore costs, we have to understand the growth strategy and how value is delivered by market segment. From earlier discussion, you will recall that to increase volume, CSC decided the following:

- Grow in the custom door market segment.
- Grow in the semicustom door market segment.
- Investigate the standard door market segment since growth is below average and has a lower margin.

Grow in custom door market segment: Figure 5.1 shows how value is delivered in the custom door market segment. Once the doors are produced in Asia by the suppliers, the doors are received by CSC and stored in the warehouse. When the materials requirement planning (MRP) system at CSC shows the doors as available, a production order is released to pull the doors, inspect and sand the doors, and ship them to the distributor. The lead time between a purchase order placed at the supplier to availability at CSC is about 60 days. The lead time between custom doors arriving at CSC to processing at CSC to receiving delivery at the distributor is about 10 days. Once the distributor gets the custom door order, they place the doors in their warehouse. Once their MRP shows that the doors are available and based on the builder requirement dates, the doors are pulled, subject to fine sanding and staining the doors, applying locksets, and shipping the doors to the construction site.

As the CSC team pass through the value chain, they realize some quick-win opportunities. Why should CSC receive the custom doors at the CSC facility? The custom doors are custom produced by the supplier with specific wood, design, glass, and so forth, and the entire order is meant to be for one customer. The only risk management activity that CSC operations was providing was to inspect for any deep scratches or damaged products. Historical quality records indicate that over the last 5 years, those instances were rare, and this is not a common problem. Once a custom door order is placed with the supplier, if the supplier can ship directly to the distributor, the lead time for the order can be reduced to about 10 days from the current 70 days. In Figure 5.1, steps 18–20 and the freight cost to the distributor can be eliminated, leading to higher profitability for CSC. A quick estimate by the team shows that they can reduce the cost by about $400 per order. To make this change successful, the CSC supply chain team needs to negotiate with suppliers on shipping to distributors directly and provide CSC boxes to the supplier so that they can ship the custom doors in them. Since all suppliers of CSC have noncompete agreements with CSC, they cannot do business directly with the distributors in the future. The CSC sales team needs to communicate to the distributors that custom orders will be shipped directly from suppliers to improve on-time delivery. If you recall, from the voice of the customer (VOC) study, the CSC team learned that on-time delivery is one of the top three factors for choosing a custom door manufacturer. By eliminating 10 days in the value chain, CSC will have these 10 days as a buffer to ensure that products are delivered on time and achieve a greater than 95% delivery performance. Note that CSC is still communicating the original lead time to customers, though they have removed 10 days of lead time in processing

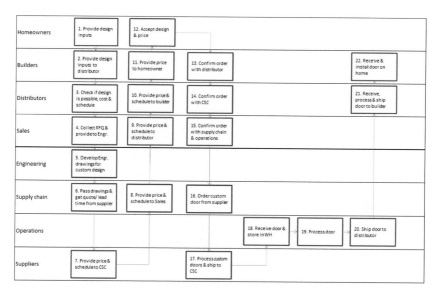

FIGURE 5.1
Process map for delivering value in the custom door market segment.

an order. Since order lead time is not the top driver in selecting a custom door based on the survey, CSC is not communicating a lower lead time to customers; instead, they are using the reduced processing time to ensure better delivery to customers. Based on the VOC study conducted, CSC has learned that on-time delivery is one of the key factors for selecting the manufacturer. Making this change will eliminate the noncore costs of receiving, storing, picking, inspecting, repackaging, and freight to customers, while achieving the growth strategy for custom doors.

Grow in semicustom door market segment: Figure 5.2 shows how value is delivered in the semicustom door market segment. Once an order is confirmed from the customer, the doors are pulled from the warehouse, minor customization work is performed, and the doors are sanded and shipped to the customer.

"More customization options" was among the feedback from the VOC study for this market segment. From the customer relationship management (CRM) system at CSC, the marketing team knows the customization options requested by customers. So the CSC team decides to introduce more customization options by making the following changes:

- New glass, panel carvings, and molding designs are added as options.
- Builders can provide custom glass for CSC to install.

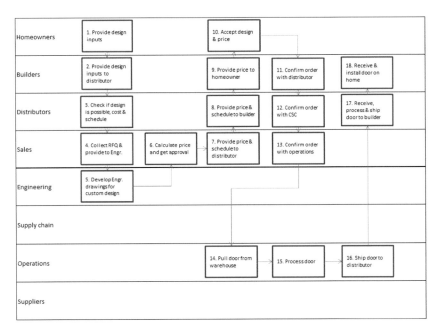

FIGURE 5.2
Process map for delivering value in the semicustom door market segment.

- The sales, marketing, and operations teams identify more minor customization options to be provided, such as drilling of peep holes, hardware location, and weather strips.
- The fastest-growing builders in the market are identified and more customization features are provided specifically to these customers.

Another major factor for growth in the semicustom door market was ease of doing business. As you can see, the ease of doing business is very subjective. So in order to understand better, the CSC team interviews some customers further to understand how they can improve doing business with them. Two major challenges evolve from the interviews—a simple way to customize the doors and accurate billing. In order to simplify the customizing and ordering process, an Internet portal is created for select customers to select all the options for customization by themselves and submit the order or request for quote. CSC decides to start with select customers so that they can learn and scale up to other customers. Regarding accurate billing, most of the root causes are due to inaccurate payment terms or inaccurate pricing. The Internet portal will solve the pricing problem. Later in the working capital section, we will learn how the problem of inaccurate payment terms is solved.

Investigate standard door market: Since the growth rate of the standard door market segment is below average, and the profit margins are lower, CSC has to investigate if the investments in this market segment make sense. From Table 5.2, we can see that the cost of setting up a warehouse on the West Coast, to increase the sales of standard doors, is about 2% of sales. In the past, the management team had believed that the standard door market would grow substantially and, to penetrate the West Coast, they should set up this distribution center. The cost of 2% of sales is only for the increase in freight and lease of the warehouse; it does not include the cost of operating the warehouse and the personnel there. There are 20 employees in that warehouse. Table 5.3 shows the operating expense of the warehouse. The CSC team decides that the cost is not justified. Since growing the standard door market segment is not a primary growth strategy for the company, the CSC team feels confident in closing this warehouse and supporting the West Coast sales from the factory. This will yield an additional $2 million increase in profit.

3. OPTIMIZE CORE COSTS

After eliminating or reducing the noncore costs of the business, the core costs should be addressed. Remember, core cost only means that the activity is required to achieve the company objectives. However, the costs for core activities can always be improved. To optimize the costs of the business, CSC walks through each cost category and identifies opportunities for improvement.

TABLE 5.3

West Coast Warehouse Expenses

	Current Year
Lease	$840,000
Freight	$350,000
Warehouse expense	$50,000
Employee expense	$800,000
Total	**$2,040,000**

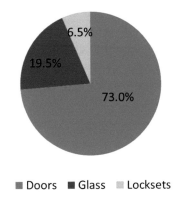

FIGURE 5.3
Annual spend by commodity for direct materials.

Direct material: For most manufacturing companies, the cost of direct materials represents about 30%–70% of sales. In order to improve the direct material cost, companies should investigate:

- Cost per unit from supplier
- Better usage of material to reduce scrap
- Alternate materials that give better or equal performance at a lower cost

For CSC, the total spend on direct materials represents about 43% of sales. Direct materials consist of doors, door blanks, glass inserts, and door locksets. Figure 5.3 shows the annual direct material spend by commodity. As we can see, more than 73% of the direct material spend is for door suppliers. So CSC will decide to focus attention on door suppliers for optimizing costs.

Figure 5.4 shows the annual spend by door supplier. As shown, CSC has added several door manufacturers over the years. As a result, CSC has not focused their spend on a handful of suppliers to leverage their buying capacity. Some of the door suppliers have access to certain unique woods; hence, the spend is low with these suppliers, but CSC still needs to do business with them.

Ideally, a company should be able to give all the business to one supplier and expect a huge volume discount. But there are several factors that limit this approach. Some of the limiting factors are risk management, supplier capacity, and supplier capabilities.

Annual spend by door supplier

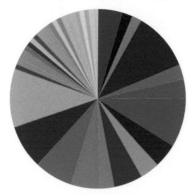

FIGURE 5.4
Annual spend by door supplier.

In order to improve on the door buying costs, CSC takes a strategic approach. They evaluate the need for doing business with the supplier along with the supplier's operating performance over the last 3 years. CSC develops a strategic supplier assessment scorecard. Table 5.4 shows this scorecard for CSC. Each supplier is evaluated based on unique wood offerings, unique design offerings, delivery performance, quality performance, and ease of doing business. Price is not considered a factor since it can be easily changed by any supplier based on volume. For each of the evaluation criteria, a supplier is given a score between 1 and 5. The supplier score (last column) is obtained by multiplying the score for each of the evaluation criteria. So the higher the supplier score, the more valuable a supplier is to do business. For example, supplier 1 has the following scores:

- Unique wood = 1
- Unique design = 5
- Delivery = 5
- Quality = 3
- Ease of business = 1

So the evaluation of supplier 1 is that the supplier has no unique wood offering but has some unique design offerings for custom design; delivery is above 95% on time; quality is between 85% and 90%; and the supplier is not easy to do business with. As you can see, the higher the supplier score,

TABLE 5.4

Strategic Supplier Assessment Scorecard

Supplier	Unique Wood	Unique Design	Delivery	Quality	Ease of Business	Supplier Score
1	1	5	5	3	1	75
2	2	3	4	5	5	600
3	1	1	2	3	5	30
4	3	1	5	5	5	375
5	1	3	3	4	1	36
6	1	2	4	5	5	200
7	3	5	5	4	5	1500
8	3	2	4	5	5	600
9	1	2	5	5	5	250
10	1	5	4	4	3	240
11	5	1	3	4	3	180
12	1	4	5	4	4	320
13	1	3	4	4	2	96
14	1	5	5	5	3	375
15	1	2	4	5	1	40
16	3	3	5	5	5	1125
17	4	3	5	5	5	1500
18	2	5	3	5	4	600
19	3	4	5	5	5	1500
20	4	3	4	5	4	960
21	3	3	2	4	5	360
22	2	3	4	5	5	600
23	1	3	5	5	3	225
24	2	4	5	5	5	1000
25	3	3	2	3	2	108
26	5	5	3	5	3	1125
27	1	4	4	3	5	240
28	1	2	4	3	4	96
29	1	1	4	4	3	48
30	1	1	5	3	5	75
31	1	1	5	4	2	40
32	1	1	4	5	5	100
33	1	2	3	4	5	120
34	1	3	3	3	5	135
35	5	2	2	3	4	240
36	1	3	5	5	5	375

the more strategic or important the supplier is to CSC. Suppliers with low scores are not strategic.

As the CSC supply chain team assembles the strategic supplier assessment scorecard, they discuss the true capabilities and limitations of each supplier. After this analysis, CSC selects eight suppliers as their future strategic suppliers. These eight suppliers can cover all the designs and woods and have performed excellently over the years. The next step is for the CSC supply chain team to work with these suppliers to negotiate new pricing based on increased volume and transfer the work to them. The CSC team feels confident that they can achieve price reduction and reduce the direct material spend from 43% of sales to 40% of sales. This adds 3% of earnings before interest and tax (EBIT) to CSC. Hence, optimizing the core cost of direct materials can make a significant improvement to CSC's profitability.

Direct labor: In manufacturing companies, direct labor typically represents 3%–20% of sales. In order to improve direct labor cost, companies should investigate:

- Classic industrial engineering techniques of motion studies and eliminating non-value-added tasks
- Automation, which has delivered significant productivity gains over the last three decades
- Outsourcing or offshoring of manufacturing operations, which captures the labor cost arbitrage

Figure 5.5 shows the process flow for a typical door in CSC. Each door segment is different based on customization level, market segment, finishing, and so forth. As the orders flow through each process, it may get held up for 1–3 days between processes. When this high-level flow was reviewed with the team, the sales team questioned the need for

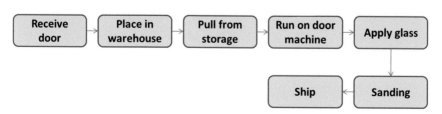

FIGURE 5.5
Process flow for a typical door in CSC.

sanding. When the distributors receive the doors, they place them in their warehouse. When the distributors are ready to process the doors at their facility, the first action that they perform is thorough and detailed sanding. The detailed sanding is a prerequisite for staining the doors. So the value of sanding at CSC was questionable. Only when there are deep gashes on the door is sanding in a sand booth necessary. Quality records indicate that less than 1% of the doors have deep marks. So the CSC team decides to eliminate the sanding operation for all doors. However, after applying glass the operators will visually inspect if there are any deep gashes. Only if there are deep gashes will the operators sand the specific marks with a sanding machine in the sanding booth.

The total labor time spent in moving a door to the sanding booth, sanding the door, and bringing the door back to the workstation is about 30 minutes per door. Since CSC processes about 25,000 doors in a year, the labor cost saved from selective sanding is 25,000 × 0.5 hours × $20 per hour = $250,000. This represents about 0.4% of EBIT improvement to CSC.

In addition to labor cost improvement, there is a reduction in production lead time. In the current process at CSC, after applying glass by an operator, the door is set aside and the production shop order is closed. This indicates to the production scheduler that the door is ready for the next operation, that is, sanding. Then the scheduler releases another shop order to process the door in the sanding booth. A material handler then moves this door to the sanding booth queue. One of the sanding booth operators pulls the door and then sands it. After sanding, the production operator sets the door aside and closes the shop order. This again indicates to the scheduler that the door is ready to be moved for shipping. The lead time between applying glass and the door being ready to ship can vary from 2 to 5 days in the current process. With the introduction of conditional sanding, the lead time is reduced to less than 1 day. This represents a reduction in the work in process and customer lead time for the semicustom door market.

Also, from the earlier discussion of the custom door market segment, we can eliminate the entire production process for this market segment from CSC. If custom doors are shipped directly from the supplier to the distributor, then the whole process of receiving and processing can be eliminated from CSC, which could lead to an additional 0.2% improvement in EBIT from direct labor. Hence, the total improvement in EBIT from direct labor is 0.6%.

Indirect material: The cost of material required to support production can vary from 1% to 5% of sales. In order to improve the direct material cost, companies should investigate:

- Cost per unit from supplier
- Better usage of material to reduce scrap
- Alternate materials that give better or equal performance at a lower cost

With the introduction of conditional sanding at CSC, there is indirect material savings of sanding paper and sanding tools. Also, there is indirect material savings in electricity cost since the sanding booths have high-power vacuum pumps that suck out all the dust that comes from sanding the doors. Additionally, the cost of filters for the four sanding booths also adds up to a significant cost for indirect materials. After the changes, CSC can operate the business with only one sanding booth. Based on the changes in the process, the CSC team feels confident that they can improve the EBIT by 0.5%.

Indirect labor: The CSC team chooses not to make any immediate changes to indirect labor since there is a lot of effort required to implement all the changes. CSC will need the indirect headcount to drive the improvement activities identified.

Freight: Depending on the industry, freight costs can vary from 2% to 8% of sales. Freight costs can be reduced by better price negotiation with the freight forwarder, shipping full truckloads, avoiding expediting freight charges, and so forth.

CSC realizes that there are two initiatives that have already been discussed that will reduce freight cost. First, the direct shipment of custom doors from the supplier to the distributor can eliminate freight cost incurred by CSC. Second, closing the West Coast warehouse also will eliminate the freight cost from the factory to the distribution center. CSC looks at their logistics data and realizes that they can improve the EBIT by 0.2%.

Other manufacturing expenses: The CSC team chooses not to make any changes to this cost driver at this time.

SG&A: SG&A cost can vary from 3% to 20% for most manufacturing companies. SG&A comprises executive salaries, salaried wages, marketing and selling expenses, and so forth. In order to achieve maximum profitability, the SG&A costs have to be optimal. The fastest way to reduce

SG&A cost is to reduce headcount; however, this could impact a company's growth aspirations. Before making any changes to the SG&A structure of a business, it is good to understand the company's strategy and make sure that it is aligned.

The CSC team decides not to make any significant changes to the SG&A structure to reduce costs. This is because CSC wants to rapidly grow the business as discussed in earlier chapters. Since the CSC team decided to grow in the custom and semicustom market segments, they want to make sure the SG&A costs are aligned to that vision. Recall that in order to grow in the custom market, the VOC study suggested that CSC needs to provide fast designs/quotes and exclusive designs. Of course, the team can map the design/quote process and see how they can streamline it. A quick solution that was provided was to add an engineer dedicated to providing quotes and designs for the custom door market. The current engineers were shared among all market segments and were working on quotes on a first-in, first-out basis. Having a dedicated engineer ensures that he or she can quickly get back to the customers of the custom door market. Also, since CSC decided to grow this market segment, adding an engineer ensures that CSC is ready for growth and does not cause customer relationship issues. The added engineer can learn CSC's business and be prepared to meet the growing demand in the custom and semicustom market segments.

In order to develop exclusive designs, which is also feedback from the VOC study, CSC decides to hire a temporary designer. This designer will develop exclusive designs for homeowners based on design trends. Their designs can be provided from CSC to builders so that they can offer them to the homeowners. CSC has tried some designers in the past and was very successful in pricing those doors at a premium.

No other changes will be made to the SG&A costs at this point. So the cost of adding one engineer and one part-time designer increases the SG&A cost by $200,000. Therefore, this increased SG&A cost reduces EBIT by 0.3%.

Other expenses: The CSC team chooses not to make any changes to this cost driver at this time.

Figure 5.6 shows the EBIT bridge for CSC with the cost optimization actions. If the volume remains the same in CSC, the EBIT margin for CSC increases from 14.7% to 22.3%. This represents a 51% increase in EBIT margin for CSC.

Figure 5.6 shows the EBIT margin assuming the same volume in CSC. However, CSC is growing its top line by increasing volume and pricing.

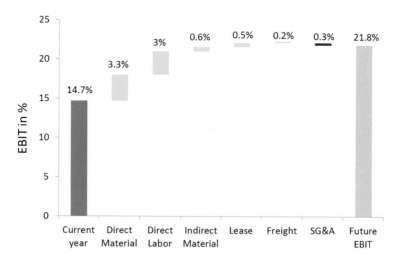

FIGURE 5.6
EBIT margin with same volume.

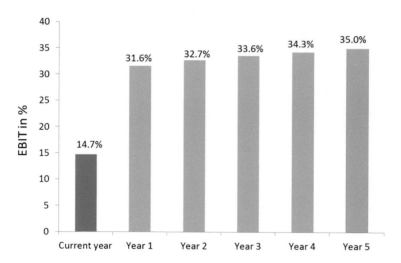

FIGURE 5.7
EBIT forecast with increased volume and pricing.

Hence, the EBIT margin for CSC is much higher. Figure 5.7 shows the EBIT margin for CSC with higher volume and pricing based on the actions of the CSC team. The ramp-up from the current year to year 1 may vary slightly due to the time required for sales to ramp up. But beyond year 1, the forecast should be accurate. The three-step cost optimization roadmap can yield significant improvement in margin expansion.

As shown above, cost can be improved by:

1. Understanding the cost drivers
2. Identifying and eliminating noncore costs
3. Optimizing core costs

Practical Tips

- Engage the marketing/sales teams in the cost optimization brainstorming and related activities. This will ensure that you have their support, alignment, and input to improve since they understand value from the customer perspective.
- You may have to normalize costs to per unit of volume instead of revenue. This is especially true in industries with varying commodity raw material prices.
- The perspective on noncore costs may vary by company depending on the maturity of the organization.
- The breakout of cost categories for trending may vary by company. Start at a high level and get the details as applicable.
- For process mapping, always walk the process and make actual observations. Do not get "experts" in a conference room and try to map, as this will only give you the map for how the process should ideally work.
- If a process is noncore but necessary, consider outsourcing so other companies can manage the nuances of these processes.
- Use creativity to solve process and cost problems before investing in automation and machines.
- When making improvements to cost, consider the impact on process lead time and working capital.
- Always aim for simplicity of processes; this will lead to lower cost and not vice versa.
- The low-price supplier may not be the low-cost supplier. Never give up on quality and level of service for the hope of a low invoice price from a supplier. Make sure that you understand the total landed cost and total operating cost of a product from your supplier.
- Keep your request for proposal (RFP) process simple from suppliers. You do not have to invest in lots of technology tools to get bids from suppliers.

- While rationalizing suppliers, remember to have an optimum number of suppliers. Do not commit all your business to one supplier since this could cause supply risk.
- Minimize handoffs and simplify processes to reduce cost. The hidden cost of coordinating handoffs and disconnects is usually not visible on a financial statement. However, when you walk the process, this becomes apparent.
- Utilize technology and social media to reduce advertising expenses.
- Companies should identify activities to outsource that do not add value and are not core to the company's operations.
- Explore dual-sourcing strategies for high-spend direct materials. Depending on the supplier performance level, move a share of the wallet to the better-performing supplier to ensure that suppliers understand the value of good performance to your company.

6

Working Capital: The Right Grade of Fuel

Every business requires some level of capital investment. For the capital invested, businesses should provide sustainable returns while minimizing risk. Shareholders have a choice in investing their capital among several investment options. Different investment options carry varying levels of risk and returns for the investor. So every business should ensure that they provide the maximum sustainable return to their investors to remain an attractive choice for investing. Return on invested capital (ROIC) is one of the most important metrics that managers should control to create value for the firm. Hence, investment of capital in businesses by business leaders should be well thought out.

The capital from investors can be used for multiple reasons. Capital may be deployed to set up factories, develop new products, hire employees, carry inventory, and so forth. Capital is used not only to grow the profitability of the firm, but also to prevent risks to the company, such as machine guarding, buffer stock, and emission controlling equipment. The business leaders decide on the optimum use of capital to achieve the company's strategy while providing the maximum return to the investors on a sustainable basis.

To improve the value of a company, the company needs to generate sufficient free cash flow from its operations. Higher profit is good, but cash is king. Free cash flow is revenue minus operating costs and long-term investment on capital items or investment in securities. Working capital is an indicator of the efficiency of management of investment. Most of the factors, such as interest rates and securities, are not controlled frequently by profit and loss (P&L) owners. The best way for P&L owners to improve cash flow from operations is to improve their working capital required and fixed assets to operate the business.

The performance of working capital can be measured by normalizing the dollar value. Having a trade working capital of $10 million may not mean much since we do not know if this is the working capital required to support a $12 million or $100 million business. Hence, working capital as a percentage of sales is more valuable to understanding the efficiency of the management of capital in a business.

For illustration purposes, CSC's working capital is composed only of inventory, accounts receivable, and accounts payable. We will not take other factors into account, such as vendor financing or foreign exchange. We will also not consider fixed asset rationalization for this discussion.

CSC working capital

= Inventory $ + Accounts Receivables $ − Accounts Payables $

The performance of CSC's working capital as a percentage of sales is about 33%, with a target of 28%. The largest driver of working capital for CSC is accounts receivable, followed by inventory. The average values are:

- Inventory = $12.1 million
- Accounts receivable = $14.8 million
- Accounts payable = $6 million

The CSC team sets a target to achieve a trade working capital level that is below 28% of sales. The additional free cash flow generated can be returned to the shareholders or used to either reduce debt or fund growth of the company.

INVENTORY

Before addressing how we can optimize the inventory level, let us understand the merits and risks of carrying inventory in a business.

The availability of inventory provides several benefits to a business:

- Flexibility in meeting customer demand
- Buffer for production and supply chain issues
- Ability to win new business on the agreement of carrying inventory dedicated to the customer
- Shorter lead times for customer orders

However, having excess inventory also causes problems to the business:

- Ties up cash
- Hides production and supply chain issues
- Builds complacency in the organization
- Requires more storage space
- Requires more warehouse personnel
- Creates a risk of inventory damage
- Increases inventory shrinkage
- Increases insurance

The key is to optimize the level of inventory based on customer needs and operations processes. Reducing inventory is easy—just stop building it, but this will lead to unsatisfied customers, reduced sales, and eventually losses to the business. Inventory optimization can be achieved by taking the steps below.

1. Categorize inventory levels over time.
2. Segment inventory based on variability of demand and inventory value.
3. Develop an inventory management strategy for each segment.
4. Identify inventory stocking levels.

1. Categorize Inventory Levels Over Time

The benefits of categorizing inventory levels over time are:

- Help identify areas to focus on
- Identify seasonality
- Identify any special causes for spikes or drops in inventory levels

Before starting any analysis, we have to note that CSC is a make-to-order production system. So doors are not produced unless a firm order is received from the customer. This is in contrast to a make-to-stock production system, where the finished goods are produced to maintain certain stock levels. Only the standard doors sold out of the West Coast distribution center are currently make to stock. The custom doors are considered made-to-engineer products since they are designed, sourced, and produced specifically to a customer's requirements.

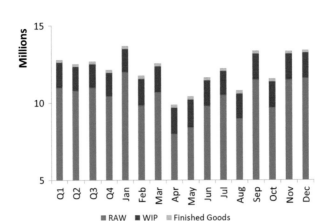

FIGURE 6.1
CSC inventory levels for last 12 months.

Figure 6.1 shows the inventory levels at CSC over the last 12 months and the average inventory by quarter 2 years ago. Note that it does not include the custom door market segment. The reason custom doors are excluded from CSC is because we know that in the future these doors will be completely finished from the suppliers and shipped directly to distributors. As shown, the average inventory for CSC is about $12.1 million. There is no seasonality in this business. The biggest opportunity lies in reducing raw material inventory. Remember, CSC buys door blanks from their suppliers in Southeast Asia with a lead time of about 60 days. Work in process (WIP) represents the second largest opportunity to reduce inventory. CSC carries minimal finished goods since most doors are processed only when an order is available from the customer. Based on this information, the CSC team decides to focus on optimizing the inventory levels categorized as raw material and WIP. With the closure of the West Coast distribution facility, some of the finished goods inventory will decrease.

Based on previous discussion on streamlining production flow, the WIP level in the plant should reduce by about 50%. This change results in free cash flow of about $800,000. The reduction in WIP by $800,000 represents an approximate 5-day reduction in days of inventory on hand.

2. Segment Inventory Based on Variability of Demand and Inventory Value

To improve the raw material inventory, CSC looks at the last 12 months of actual performance and the forecast for the next 6 months from sales. In

Part Number	Actual shipped quantity				Forecast next 6 months				Based on Actuals			Based on Forecast		
	Week 1	Week 2	---	Week 52	Week 1F	Week 2F	---	Week 26F	Average	Std. Dev	CV	Average	Std. Dev	CV

FIGURE 6.2
Data collection table to understand variability of demand.

order to do this, CSC collects data on the actual release of each door blank from the warehouse to the production floor by week. Since we are focused on raw material, we are looking at the consumption of doors from the warehouse to maintain the optimum level of inventory in the warehouse. For example, if a semicustom door was released to production on July 15, then the part number of the door blank is considered to be consumed on July 15. The data collection table is as shown in Figure 6.2.

The purpose of Figure 6.2 is to understand the variability of demand. If the demand from customers is consistent, then it is easy to plan for inventory. For example, if the demand is 100 doors of a certain part number every week, then we can receive 100 doors every week and ship them by the end of the week. However, we know in reality that not all products have consistent demand patterns.

In Figure 6.2, the CSC team looks at the actual shipments made in the last 12 months by week for each part number. They also look at the sales forecast for these part numbers in the next 6 months based on the new growth strategy for the company. Average demand by week is calculated for both the actuals and the forecast. Then the standard deviation is calculated in weekly demand separately for both the actuals and the forecast. Finally, the coefficient of variation (CV) is calculated for both the actuals and the forecast. The CV is calculated by dividing standard deviation by the average (CV = standard deviation/average).

Once the above computations are completed, the CSC team conducts a meeting with the sales, operations, finance, and supply chain teams. The purpose of the meeting is to get alignment on demand to plan the operations. If the average inventory levels of actuals and the forecast are approximately the same for a part number from the above computations, then there is no issue. However, if there is a significant difference, then the team needs to discuss why there is a difference and if this is acceptable. For example, CSC may see that the demand forecast for a certain semicustomizable door blank has increased in the forecast. The increase could exist since CSC decided to grow in the semicustom market segment. However, the supply chain team needs to make sure that the suppliers are capable of supplying and warehouse space is available, and operations need to be staffed to process the semicustomization work. Also, by only looking at past performance, we may continue to provide the same level of delivery as in the past. So we have to look at the forecast to ensure that the business is ready to support custom demand. This alignment meeting also ensures that we have agreement among all functions to either take the risk of excess inventory or reduce customer delivery.

From Figure 6.2, we use Figure 6.3 to segment inventory as shown. On the *y*-axis, we have inventory value based on standard cost multiplied by number of units sold. The A items represent the top 80% of the door blanks sold, the B items are the next 15%, and the C items are the last 5%. On the *x*-axis, we have variability of demand represented by CV. The L items have CV < 1, M items have CV between 1 and 2, and the H items have CV > 2. The higher the variability, the higher CV. So a product in AL segment means that the product represents the top 80% of consumption/sales and has low variability in weekly demand. However, a product in the CH segment means that the product has very low contribution to the company sales and has very high variability in weekly demand.

Figure 6.4 shows the inventory matrix filled with CSC data. Each segment shows the number of stock keeping units (sku) of the average inventory dollar value at the end of the week for the last 12 months, the average

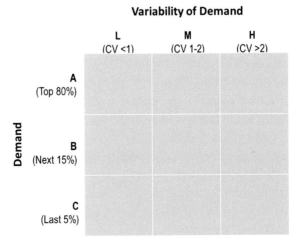

FIGURE 6.3
Inventory matrix for demand and variability.

sales or consumption for that sku, and the number of weeks of coverage. Figure 6.4 also shows "D items." D items are products that CSC carries in their warehouse that show up as raw inventory on the balance sheet but there have been no sales of the items in the last 12 months. Approximately $1 million is tied up in cash as D items in inventory.

3. Develop Inventory Management Strategy for Each Segment

Once inventory is segmented as in Figure 6.4, each segment needs to be addressed with the appropriate strategy for replenishment. Depending on the agreed-on tactics, the investment required may vary. For example, if a company decides to have point-of-sale information sent all the way to the supply chain to trigger replenishment, then the investment required in technology is much higher. It is usually better to keep the replenishment process simple and less capital-intensive.

The first quick-win opportunity would be D items. Since this is inventory with no sales in the last 12 months, the CSC team decides to either run a special promotion or sell the items back to the suppliers. This releases about $1 million in cash flow, which represents about 6 days of inventory on hand.

For A items, the CSC team decides to have a replenishment strategy with a maximum of 4 weeks of supply on hand. They can have a lower supply level at 1 week, but based on the distance of suppliers and amount of change to the organization, a 1-month period of supply will be a good

		L		M		H	
		Value	%	Value	%	Value	%
A	# of sku	28	8%	20	6%	14	4%
	Avg. inventory (week)	$ 4,000,000	33%	$ 1,420,000	12%	$ 1,300,000	11%
	Avg. sales (week)	$ 572,000	48%	$ 240,000	20%	$ 184,000	12%
	Coverage (week)	7		6		7	
B	# of sku	65	19%	75	22%	10	3%
	Avg. inventory (week)	$ 1,450,000	12%	$ 1,550,000	13%	$ 600,000	5%
	Avg. sales (week)	$ 80,000	7%	$ 71,000	6%	$ 30,000	3%
	Coverage (week)	18		22		20	
C	# of sku	20	6%	18	5%	64	19%
	Avg. inventory (week)	$ 180,000	1%	$ 100,000	1%	$ 500,000	4%
	Avg. sales (week)	$ 14,000	1%	$ 10,000	1%	$ 31,250	3%
	Coverage (week)	13		10		16	
D	# of sku	26	8%				
	Avg. inventory (week)	$ 1,040,000	9%				
	Avg. sales (week)	$ -	0%				
	Coverage (week)						

FIGURE 6.4
CSC inventory matrix for demand and variability.

starting point for CSC. So the A items will be delivered every month based on a fixed quantity. For B items, the CSC team decides to have 8 weeks of supply on hand. Finally, for C items the CSC team decides to have 13 weeks of supply on hand. This becomes the ABC inventory policy for CSC to manage inventory levels. As you can see, the inventory policy is based on inventory value and supplier lead time consideration.

For L items, meaning products with a low coefficient of variation (CV), CSC decides to have regular deliveries. The regular deliveries are similar to a milk run. A milk run is the delivery of a set quantity of parts at a regular cadence or interval. For the AL segment, products will be delivered every month based on a set quantity, which is discussed in the next step. Similarly, products in BL segment will be delivered every 2 months based on a set quantity since the B items will have 2 months of supply, as discussed above. The products in the CL segment are mostly accessory items, such as door bottom weather strips, door seals, screws, and washers. Most of these items can be placed on vendor-managed inventory. Vendor-managed inventory is an inventory management tactic where the vendor keeps the low-value products at the customer site. When the vendor places the parts at the customer site, the vendor still owns the parts. Upon pulling the parts from the vendor-managed inventory location for the customer, the customer now owns the inventory. A representative from the vendor checks the inventory levels once or twice a week and determines the amount to invoice the customers and replenishes the inventory of parts consumed. As the CSC team identifies strategic suppliers and negotiates new contracts, they will ensure that vendor-managed inventory is enforced with these suppliers.

For M items, most of the inventory value is primarily in A and B items. For these products, better forecasting can improve how the inventory can be maintained. The CSC team decides to instill a monthly forecasting meeting with the sales team and supply chain team. The purpose of this meeting is to discuss current sales pursuits, the probability of success, and expected customization. From this meeting, the supply chain team can better plan for the inventory of these products to arrive just in time from the suppliers.

For H items, the products will be managed differently based on the nature of the products. There are several tactics to manage parts in this category:

- Products such as exclusive glass could be placed on consigned inventory. By placing parts in consigned inventory, CSC does not carry the inventory on their balance sheet until it is used for production. The benefit for the glass supplier is that CSC will market the exclusive offerings of the glass supplier for carrying ready inventory on consignment.

- Some products in the H category will be managed individually on a purchase order on a purchase order basis.
- Product lead times can be extended.
- Products may have low volume, so they become good candidates for rationalization.

4. Identify Inventory Stocking Levels

From the above discussion, it becomes apparent that the inventory levels need to be determined specifically for the AL and BL segments since they will require regular replenishment. The inventory stocking level is dependent on several factors:

- Rate of customer demand
- Desired service level to customer
- Supplier lead time
- Minimum order quantity from supplier
- Supplier delivery performance
- Supplier quality performance
- Cycle time from availability on dock to the production floor

The CSC team requires a simple way to develop the inventory stocking levels for these part numbers. The formula that the CSC team uses for the AL and BL segment is:

Inventory level for a part

= Supplier lead time * {(Average weekly demand + Multiple of standard deviation of demand based on service level desired

  * Risk factor for supplier performance)}

The supplier lead time for each part can be obtained from the supplier based on the contract. The average weekly demand is already calculated in Figure 6.2. The standard deviation of demand by part is also calculated in Figure 6.2. The risk factor for the supplier performance can be evaluated based on the historical performance data of the supplier.

To achieve 95% on-time delivery, the CSC team is quick to realize that it is not necessary to achieve this for all products. Since the majority of the volume/sales (80%) is driven by A items, CSC decides to achieve 97%

on-time delivery for these products. These are the products that drive the majority of value to the business; hence, achieving delivery performance above industry levels will be attractive to customers. The B parts can be set to achieve a 90% on-time delivery, and the C parts an 80% on-time delivery. Note that the weighted average of the above will still yield the 95% on-time delivery target for CSC. The point here is to achieve higher levels of customer service for the critical few parts that drive the most value.

Depending on A, B, or C product, the multiple for standard deviation will vary. The CSC team uses a Z table to figure out the appropriate multiple to get the desired customer service level. Figure 6.5 gives an example of a part in the AL segment. This chart shows the weekly consumption rate of a part in the last 52 weeks. By consulting with a cross-functional team, the CSC team is assured that the demand pattern does not change much. As you can see, the average demand is 25.6, but there has also been a high demand of 38 doors in a week. So to achieve 97% on-time delivery, the CSC team has to maintain stock level as follows:

$$
\begin{aligned}
\text{Inventory level} =\ & \text{Supplier Lead Time} * \big\{ \big(\text{Average weekly demand} \\
& + \text{Multiple of standard deviation of demand based} \\
& \text{on service level desired} \\
& * \text{Risk factor for supplier performance} \big\} \big) \\
=\ & 4 \text{ weeks} * \big\{ (25.6 + 1.88 * 3.3 * 1.1) \big\} \\
=\ & 129.69 \sim 130 \text{ door blanks}
\end{aligned}
$$

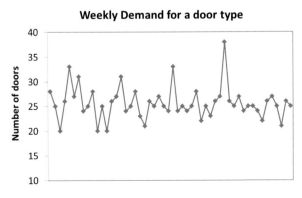

Weekly Demand for a door type

FIGURE 6.5
Weekly demand pattern for a part.

where:

4 weeks is the supplier lead time for this door blank since A parts will be delivered once a month

1.88 is the multiple factor achieving 97% on-time delivery

3.3 is the standard deviation for the weekly demand of this door blank

1.1 is the risk factor based on supplier delivery and quality performance

In a similar fashion, the inventory levels for all the parts are calculated and a process to trigger replenishment is developed by the CSC team. The process clearly highlights the inventory trigger points, roles and responsibilities, progress review cadence, process and system changes, inventory level adjustment process, and so forth. Based on the above actions for raw inventory, CSC can reduce it from an average of $10.2 million to $8 million.

SUMMARY

Figure 6.6 shows the results of the inventory optimization actions. The results represent an approximate 25% reduction in inventory while improving delivery performance to customers.

As shown above, inventory level can be optimized by:

1. Categorizing inventory levels over time
2. Segmenting inventory based on the variability of demand and inventory value

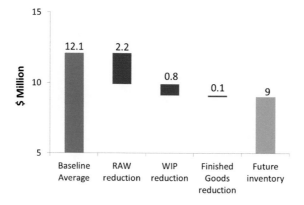

FIGURE 6.6

Summary of inventory reduction actions.

3. Developing an inventory management strategy for each segment
4. Identifying inventory stocking levels

Accounts Receivable

When a sales transaction is made, the amount of outstanding cash collection from the customer is referred to as accounts receivable (AR). Ideally, we would like to be paid first and then deliver the product. But in most business situations, the opposite is more common practice. Customers prefer longer payment terms since they can manage their cash more favorably.

The availability of AR terms provides benefits to a business:

- Being able to win new business upon the agreement of favorable terms
- Provides customers a buffer to manage their cash cycle

Like inventory, high levels of accounts receivable ties up cash for a company and reduces ROIC. Also, some industries have common practices that may limit their ability to drastically change accounts receivable terms without having a negative effect on the business.

Figure 6.7 shows the accounts receivable performance over the last 12 months.

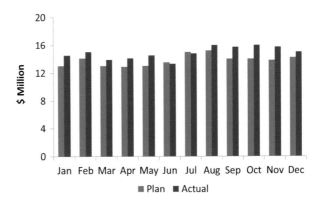

FIGURE 6.7
Accounts receivable in the last 12 months.

CSC approaches accounts receivable optimization by taking the steps below.

1. Improved execution
2. Accounts receivable cycle management
3. Accounts receivable terms rationalization
4. Technology upgrades

1. Improved Execution

Before changing the terms, CSC decides to understand how the customers are performing to current terms. There is no point in changing the terms when you cannot keep your customers accountable to existing terms. Also, CSC needs to understand why customers are not paying on time and what changes can be implemented to ensure that they do pay on time.

The CSC team looks at the last 12 months of invoices and measures whether the actual payment date matches the invoice due date. Figure 6.8 shows that about 23% of the invoices are not paid on time.

Figure 6.9 shows a histogram of number of days late. The purpose of this chart is to understand if there are any chronic issues driving late payment

Invoice Payment

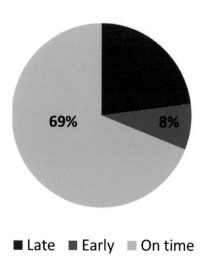

■ Late ■ Early ■ On time

FIGURE 6.8
Invoice payment in the last 12 months.

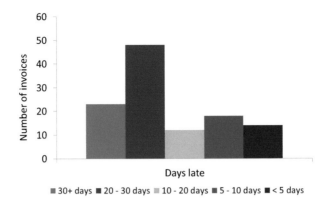

FIGURE 6.9
Accounts receivable late days in the last 12 months.

from customers. Since most invoices are more than 20 days late, the CSC team should dig further to understand the reasons. Invoices late by less than 10 days could be due to process changes, which could be addressed by looking at the accounts receivable cycle.

Upon a further deep dive, the team realizes that reasons for late payment from customers are the following:

- Invoice discrepancies
- Customers not being aware of their payment terms
- Some customers knew that they could get away with paying late since CSC did not keep them accountable

Invoice discrepancies—This was primarily driven by custom and semicustom doors. When the customers received their invoice, they had issues of the price being higher than quoted or the products being shipped before needed. The discrepancies were primarily due to a lack of a tight process from quoting to invoicing. Additionally, the CSC team agrees to introduce a price confirmation step before starting work on the order. In the price confirmation step, the customer service team sends an email to the customer's accounting/supply chain team to inform them of the product, price, and ship date—before the product is produced. This keeps the customer informed of the product coming to their warehouse and the expected price.

Customers not aware of payment terms—As the CSC sales team won new customers, several off-line agreements were made between the sales team and the customers on payment terms. This led to not only poor customer service but also a financial impact on CSC. Therefore, the leadership team at CSC decides to ensure that the sales team is informed that they cannot provide any special payment terms without CSC finance approval. Disciplinary actions will also be enforced to ensure that the right behaviors are in place. Additionally, the CSC team decides to set up an annual process where the sales leadership team sends an annual letter to the customers thanking them for their business and reminding them of their payment terms. In the price confirmation step discussed above, the payment terms will also be provided to the customers when the confirmation email is sent out.

Keeping customers accountable—In the past, CSC never strictly enforced payment terms. To ensure that CSC optimizes the use of capital, the accounts receivable team will have to strictly enforce the agreed-on payment terms with the support of the senior leadership team. This will mean that CSC will place customers on credit hold and not ship the next order and enforce late payment fees to customers who are late on payments. This will require change management with not only the customers but also the sales and operations teams within CSC. The sales team would prefer to ship to customers even though they are late so that they can still maintain a good relationship with the customers. The sales team would not prefer to inform customers that their product will not be shipped or penalties will be imposed for late payment. Similarly, the operations team would prefer to ship the product immediately after producing it. If a customer is on a credit hold, operations cannot ship the product and has more inventory than planned, which negatively affects operations' metrics. Also, when this product is shipped later, after the customer makes the payment, the order shows up as late shipment. So CSC decides to measure inventory and on-time delivery without credit holds to ensure they are not penalizing the operations team.

2. Accounts Receivable Cycle Management

Most companies look at their outstanding accounts receivable and focus a lot of time and energy in collecting them faster. Though this focus is required, easier gains can be achieved by making internal changes to the accounts receivable cycle. The accounts receivable cycle starts for most companies when the invoice is mailed to the customer. However, the time from a product shipment to the time an invoice is mailed is never captured in many companies. This is why we call this the accounts receivable cycle, meaning the total time from product shipment to cash collection. Some

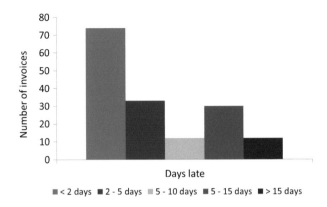

FIGURE 6.10
Days from product shipment to invoice.

companies take about 20 days to mail an invoice to the customer from the time the product is already shipped.

The CSC team conducts an analysis of days between product shipment and invoice date. The results of the analysis are shown in Figure 6.10.

As shown in Figure 6.10, about 54% of the invoices mailed take more than 2 days from the time the product is shipped. About 25% of the invoices take more than 5 days to be mailed to the customer. The average lead time to mail an invoice is 8 days.

The CSC team maps the process from the time the product is shipped to the time an invoice is mailed and finds several opportunities to reduce this lead time. The biggest changes implemented are:

- For custom and semicustom doors, get price approval from the customer before producing the product.
- Capture costs from outside suppliers in the shop production work order to avoid delays.
- Close out production work orders each day immediately after shipping the product.
- Negotiate fixed freight cost with freight-forwarding companies to simplify invoicing.
- Simplify the invoicing process to avoid unnecessary loop backs in the process.

Based on the above changes, the CSC team is confident that they can consistently mail an invoice within 2 days of product shipment. The ideal

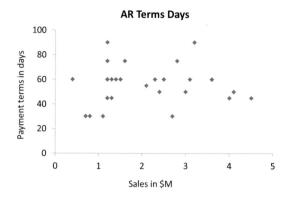

FIGURE 6.11
Sales and accounts receivable (AR) terms of each customer.

target would be to ship the invoice with the product. But achieving a consistent 2-day turnaround to have invoices mailed can improve the accounts receivable cycle significantly.

3. Accounts Receivable Terms Rationalization

Having customers on different payment terms causes higher working capital. Most times, the reasons for varied receivable terms do not really add value to the company. Simplifying the payment terms helps in optimizing working capital, customer service, and ease of management.

In reality, trying to get customers to pay earlier is not easy. Customers always prefer longer payment terms. So companies need to find the right customers to place them on earlier payment terms.

The team at CSC looks at customer payment terms along with their annual sales. The purpose of doing this analysis is to see the relative value of each customer and the payment terms offered as value. Figure 6.11 shows the payment terms and annual sales of each customer.

As shown in Figure 6.11, the median sales from customers are $1.85 million and the median accounts receivable terms are 60 days. However, as shown in zone 3, there are several customers with below-average sales but enjoying longer payment terms. Similarly, customers in zone 4 have longer payment terms. CSC decides to have a policy of AR payment terms of 45 days for customers with below median sales, and for customers with greater than median sales, the AR payment terms is 60 days. Not only does this policy improve working capital currently, but it also simplifies payment terms offered by salespeople to customers in the future.

4. Technology Upgrades

We will not discuss all the technology tools available to streamline the accounts receivable process. There are several software programs available that can autogenerate an invoice and email to the customer as soon as the product is shipped. There are also electronic data interchange (EDI) systems that can automate the invoice-to-payment process, which can significantly reduce the accounts receivable cycle time and administrative overhead. The breadth and depth of technology discussions is beyond the scope of this book. However, if companies have a sound process for invoicing, the right technology will only enhance the performance. Without a good process, trying to use technology to improve execution will not be successful.

SUMMARY

Figure 6.12 shows the results of the accounts receivable reduction actions. The results represent an approximate 38% reduction in cash tied into accounts receivable.

As shown above, accounts receivable can be improved by:

1. Improved execution
2. Accounts receivable cycle management
3. Accounts receivable terms rationalization
4. Technology upgrades

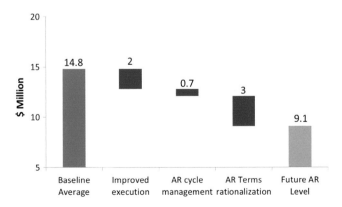

FIGURE 6.12
Summary of accounts receivable (AR) reduction actions.

Accounts Payable

Since CSC is rationalizing the number of suppliers and setting up new strategic partners, common supplier terms will be set up from the start. This will ensure optimal working capital and efficient management. The CSC team will not make any further changes for accounts payable terms now.

SUMMARY

Figure 6.13 shows the total results of working capital efforts. The reduction in working capital represents a 40% improvement from baseline, exceeding the team's goal of 20%.

For the purpose of simplicity, CSC shareholders look at the ROIC as follows:

$$ROIC = EBIT/Invested\,capital$$

$$ROIC = EBIT/(TWC + fixed\,assets)$$

Invested capital in the business is the sum of trade working capital and fixed assets. For the purpose of illustration, we will consider the fixed assets in CSC to be $45 million. With the changes implemented by the CSC team, there is minimal change to the fixed assets. So the baseline ROIC is 19.6%.

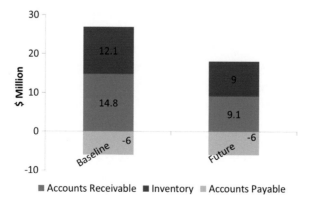

FIGURE 6.13
Results of CSC working capital improvement.

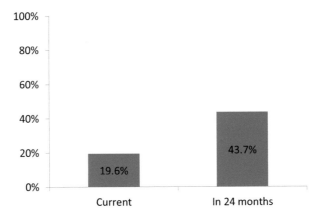

FIGURE 6.14
Results of CSC ROIC.

Based on the changes that the CSC team plans to achieve from the previous chapters, the resulting increase in ROIC is shown in Figure 6.14. The efforts from the team can lead to 2.2 times the current-state performance.

Practical Tips

- For the last 52 weeks of shipments, get data for both actual units and sales amount. This will help in identifying the actual units required to stock for inventory and cash flow impact.
- Work with suppliers to try to get inventory placed on consignment. Suppliers may be interested in carrying inventory on consignment in industries where there is high competition or a commodity product.
- Negotiate with suppliers to carry safety stock to overcome business disruptions through logistics.
- Set up two-bin or other replenishment methods with suppliers to provide a smooth demand pattern to suppliers.
- If the nature of your production is high volume and high mix, explore kitting from a third-party supplier. The process of kitting the parts for final assembly not only reduces errors in production but also could help in working capital reduction.
- Some industries may have standard payment terms as a practice for several decades, and unless you are a major player in this industry, it will be hard to change the terms.
- Reduce production lead times since this directly reduces WIP inventory.

- Measure "shipped, not invoiced" in your business. This metric will show the working capital tied up in customer orders that have been shipped but not yet invoiced.
- Develop standard invoice and payment documents. Try to avoid the intervention of customers and sales teams to create custom invoices with extra details to certain customers.
- If you have product requests from customers with poor credit rating, one way to eliminate risk and win business would be to request full or partial payment before the start of an order. This tactic will improve sales and reduce working capital.
- If you are reducing finished goods, then measure shipments for the past 52 weeks instead of release of material from the warehouse to production.
- Some businesses may require longer than a 52-week history of inventory for analysis.
- Carrying inventory for customers to deliver with a short lead time and longer payment terms can be a very effective sales strategy in some industries. However, this requires higher capital investment by companies for working capital.

7

Execution Plan: Operating Rules

Apart from developing a good transformational plan, businesses need a solid execution system to actually achieve the objectives of the plan. What is an execution system? By execution system, we are referring to operating cadence, prioritization of efforts, incentives, metrics to review progress, resource deployment, and setting a sense of urgency and importance. Though these factors may seem simple or not as important, the understanding and planning of these soft factors helps us to achieve the hard results.

Execution is where the rubber meets the road. So it is essential to document the execution plan for a major business transformation. An execution system without a business plan is like having a map but not being sure of the destination. A business plan without an execution system is like going on a journey without a map. We can all think of companies that hired high-fee consultants and MBAs who gave fancy presentations on business improvement plans. But most of these plans fail to achieve the lofty goals promised. The secret or missing link is the execution system.

The key elements of the execution system are:

1. Talent selection
2. Operating behaviors
3. Operating cadence

1. Talent Selection

Can you imagine winning a derby by betting on the wrong horse? It is the same with business; if the initiative is important to the business, you should only place your top talent as leaders or part of the initiative. The leader of the transformation should be high up in the organization and have the ear of the top executives. The leader should also have credibility in the organization by having led other key projects or initiatives in the company. If the executive team of the company does not have such a leader, then a leader from the next level of the organization should be set up to temporarily be part of the executive team. The members chosen to be part of this transformation should also be the best resources and not just the easily available resources.

At Case Study Company (CSC), the board of directors selects the general manager because of his credibility in the company. The general manager has been with the company for more than 12 years and has held key roles in finance and marketing. He has a good understanding of the market needs as well as the trends that are affecting the industry. He is also well connected with all the employees and generally looked up to by others for guidance on key business matters. Though the general manager is not part of the board of directors, he will be presenting on the progress of the transformation to the board on a regular basis.

To ensure successful execution, the general manager is given full autonomy to select the team members. The team is composed of key decision makers and subject matter experts to ensure that decisions are made based on deep knowledge of the business and the market. Most of the team members selected for this transformation will be dedicated full time for this initiative since the payback is very high. But there are some part-time participants in the transformation as well. When selecting part-time participants, clear expectations should be set with the employee and his or her manager in terms of the time and deliverables commitment. Part-time participants should view this project deliverables transformation as either equal to or more important than their current full-time role's responsibilities.

2. Operating Behaviors

When major transformations are undertaken in businesses, not everything will go smoothly. Challenges arise in execution due to missed timelines, resources changing, uncovering new issues, and so forth. As these hurdles arise, team members and executives tend to get frustrated and start blaming each other. This blame game in turn leads to lower morale, which again impacts missed timelines and plans. Once the team engagement is lost, this leads to a disengagement vortex and eventually projects fail. As the world heavyweight boxing champion Mike Tyson said, "Everyone has a plan until they get punched in the face." It is important to understand that roadblocks will erupt during any major change, but we have to be mentally prepared to react.

While taking on a major change initiative such as a business transformation, it is important to lay out the expected operating behaviors among the team members. Having simple rules that everyone can relate to makes it easy to understand and incorporate. Not only the team members, but also the sponsors and champions for these initiatives have to be aligned on these operating behaviors.

As a team exercise, CSC aligns on the following key operating behaviors:

- Always look for learning opportunities, whether a milestone is achieved or missed.
- Make positive assumptions about people when challenges occur.
- Trust but verify the changes implemented.
- There are no bad ideas or thoughts, so always bring up all the facts.

3. Operating Cadence

Some senior leaders assume that if they develop clear goals and deploy the right resources for a problem, they will get the expected results. Some also believe that if you set up regular conference calls to review project status, you can ensure change will occur. These conference calls end up being either "attaboy" or "ass-kicking" sessions depending on whether the project is making progress or not. The real problems of execution and underlying business are not discussed. Most importantly, these reviews miss out on the coaching and learning opportunities for the team members and executives.

To ensure a successful transformation, the business should set up a regular cadence of progress review and next steps at multiple levels of the organization. The frequency of reviews will vary depending on the participants and the purpose of the review. For example, the engineering team of the project may meet daily to review the progress thus far achieved by each engineer, the impact on the timelines of other engineers on the team, and key messages to deliver. However, the C-level of the organization may only want to review the project once a month to understand progress, resources required, and impact on earnings.

A common failure that we notice is that the top executives set up a regular cadence to review progress with the team leader; however, they are not sure how the subteams review progress and how the communication goes up the chain. As the leader of a transformation, he or she should ensure that they are comfortable with the progress reviews at all levels of the team and that risks and opportunities are being brought to the surface on an expedited path.

At CSC, the executive sponsor review is set up once a month with a key focus on the following:

- Milestones achieved
- Next steps
- Risks
- Resources required
- Financial impact

The weekly all-hands team review is set up with the general manager leading the discussion on the following:

- Progress of each team
- Impact analysis on overall schedule
- Risks and mitigation plans
- Resources required
- Financial impact

Each team in turn sets up two meetings per week to review the following:

- Progress achieved
- Deadlines missed
- Recovery plans
- Shifting of resources
- Risks and mitigation actions

As discussed above, the execution of a business transformation requires deliberate thought beyond just metrics and data. The complete operating environment should be documented and established to ensure success. The elements of the operating environment may not seem bigger than the financial results of a company; however, to get to the financial results, you should first focus on the operating environment before starting. The key elements of the execution system become the foundation on which you build your business transformation plan.

Practical Tips

- If the business transformation is at a business division level, then the CEO and his staff should take a couple of days to discuss and document the key elements of the execution system. If the business transformation is at the entire company level, then the board of directors should do the same exercise as above.
- Sometimes bringing an experienced turnaround leader from outside the company may help. However, for changes to stick and transformation to be successful, the sponsors of the change initiative should still plan through the business execution elements.
- If the company has certain corporate values and behaviors, then you can use them as operating behaviors as long as they are pretty specific and not too fluffy.
- Some of the senior-level reviews should be conducted face-to-face as opposed to via teleconferences. This creates direct connection to the team and shows the support of the sponsors.
- The dashboards used for progress review should be simple and easy to read.
- Align incentives to project members that clearly relate to the business transformation results. Giving stock options to key members of the team creates more ownership and responsibility to the team members.
- Always maintain a high sense of urgency in driving change.
- Set up a conference room or wall where all the subteam dashboards are displayed to conduct progress reviews.

8

Summary

For the purpose of simplicity, Case Study Company (CSC) shareholders look at return on invested capital (ROIC) as follows:

$$ROIC = EBIT/Invested\ capital$$

$$ROIC = EBIT/(TWC + fixed\ assets)$$

Invested capital in the business is the sum of trade working capital and fixed assets. For the purpose of illustration, we will consider the fixed assets of CSC to be $45 million. With the changes implemented by the CSC team, there is minimal change to the fixed assets. So the baseline ROIC is 19.6%.

Based on the changes that the CSC team plans to achieve from the previous chapters, the resulting increase in ROIC is shown in Figure 8.1. The efforts from the team can lead to 2.2 times the current-state performance.

Transforming a business's performance is a challenging endeavor. In the business world, we see more examples of failures than success. But the application of a structured and commonsense approach can increase the odds of success. The key is to keep common sense turned on. Most companies tend to blindly copy the exact steps taken in a company or industry to apply at another company or industry. Unfortunately, that leads to failure or mediocre results. Asking the fundamental questions to understand the business and solving for them leads to a good transformation plan.

As you may have observed, the approach taken in each chapter can apply to any industry. Though the nature of challenges faced by each company may vary, the structured approach with the right team will ensure that you are tackling the right obstacles. There are other key ingredients to

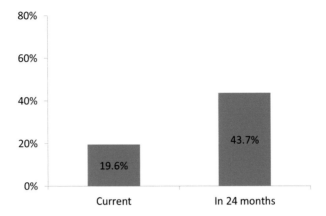

FIGURE 8.1
Results of CSC ROIC.

ensure success, such as talent management, capital allocation, and debt structuring, which are not covered in this book. But one of the most important and foundational factors for success—the approach for a transformation—is well illustrated in this book.

To improve your success rate, below are some key factors.

- Ensure that the transformation is being led by a top-level leader in the company with clout.
- While having a comprehensive transformation plan is necessary, make sure that the execution is focused and phased.
- Create a sense of urgency for execution.
- Set up an executive review committee to ensure that progress is achieved and roadblocks are eliminated on a regular basis.
- Expedite the resource allocation for the transformation projects.
- Place only the best talent in the team for the transformation journey.
- Align behaviors, metrics, actions, and results to compensation.
- Keep communication clear and often to all employees. You will notice people coming up and providing ideas to improve.
- Achieve quick wins early in the transformation so that employees can start seeing the results.

Business transformation should be a continuous process and not a one-time event. Setting a compelling vision or stretch target for the business and supporting the team to achieve the vision can lead to significant shareholder and customer gains. Note that a transformational plan goal is different from the year-over-year budget goals of 3% increase in sales, 5% increase in profit, and so forth. We are talking about setting highly compelling shifts in business performance. When the employees of a business are involved in a series of business transformations, their confidence grows. As the employees' confidence grows, they will look for more challenging targets. This is how top talent is groomed in an organization. Data shows that when you have an engaged workforce with common goals and the employees feel that they are making a contribution to the overall success of a company, turnover is lower. An agile culture creates an operating environment where the employees can quickly deal with change and adapt. Every 2 or 3 years a new goal can be established for the leaders that is beyond making monthly shipments, which could lead to series of business transformations. A company that goes through a major transformation, as shown in this case study, can have a competitive advantage in the marketplace. But when a company goes through multiple business transformations over a few years, the company becomes the clear choice for customers, shareholders, and job seekers. Sometimes developing a holistic business transformation plan as shown in this book can be broken down into phases of execution that can be executed over several years. There should always be a germ of continuous business transformation growing in the company culture. When the employees are constantly thinking and taking actions to transform the business, when changes happen in the external environment due to technology, new competition, regulations, and so forth, there is no problem in dealing with these challenges. Employees will look at those challenges as an opportunity to engage in another transformational endeavor to achieve another victory.

The business transformation roadmap discussed in this book can also be used to integrate acquisitions and create value to the stakeholders. Most companies that are acquired are apprehensive of the intent and actions of the acquiring company. As a result, this leads to withholding useful information, delay of synergies, and loss of talent. By engaging the members of the acquired company through the business transformation process, the acquiring company can create a positive work environment, build trust, and realize the financials benefits of the acquisition.

We encourage our readers to get started on their journey of business transformation in their own organizations. Every establishment has its own challenges and needs, which leads to a unique journey that the team needs to endeavor, which in turn yields a specific transformation plan for that organization. Professionals that excel at their profession are also disciples of their discipline. As the team of professionals work through their process of discovery, prioritization, and execution, they create memorable experiences and significant impact to the economy. The key is to get started. Good luck!

Index

A

Accounts receivable, 14, 60, 70–71, 72
    cycle management, 73–75, 76
    terms rationalization, 75
Accounts payable, 14, 60, 77
ASP, *see* Average selling price (ASP)
Average selling price (ASP), 26, 27, 30, 32, 33, 34

B

Blackberry, *see* Research in Motion
Business performance, 11–14, 89
Business transformation, 1–7, 10, 14, 43, 81, 83, 84–85, 89; *see also specific entries*
    Blackberry, 1
    Case Study Company (CSC), 5
    chief executive officer (CEO), 1
    chief operating officer (COO), 1
    Mergers and acquisitions (M&A), 1
    profit and loss (P&L), 1
    Research in Motion (RIM), 1

C

CAGR, *see* Compounded annual growth rate (CAGR)
Case Study Company (CSC), 5, 7–10, 12, 14, 82–84, 87, 88
    cost optimization and, 40–54
    earnings before interest and tax (EBIT), 9
    numerical control (CNC), 7
    requests for quote (RFQs), 7
    revenue growth and, 15–37
    working capital, 60, 62–69, 71–78
CEO, *see* Chief executive officer (CEO)
Chief executive officer (CEO), 1, 85
Chief operating officer (COO), 1
Coefficient of variation (CV), 63

Compounded annual growth rate (CAGR), 16, 17, 18, 20, 21, 35
COO, *see* Chief operating officer (COO)
Cost optimization, 39–57
    core costs, 47–57
    drivers, 40–42
        selling, general, administrative (SG&A), 41
    noncore costs, 43–47
        customer relationship management (CRM), 45
        materials requirement planning (MRP), 44
        voice of the customer (VOC), 44
CRM, *see* Customer relationship management (CRM)
CSC, *see* Case Study Company (CSC)
Custom door market segment, 9, 16, 17, 18, 22–26, 28, 29, 31, 32, 35, 43–45, 52–54, 61, 62
Customer relationship management (CRM), 45
CV, *see* Coefficient of variation (CV)

E

Earnings before interest and tax (EBIT), 9, 10, 16, 17–18, 35, 36, 52–56
EBIT, *see* Earnings before interest and tax (EBIT)
Execution plan, 81–85
    operating behaviors, 82–83
    operating cadence, 83–85
    talent selection, 81–82

I

Investment, 4, 9, 23, 42, 47, 59, 65, 79
Inventory, 14, 60, 73, 78, 79
    levels, over time, 61–62
    management strategy, 65–67

stocking levels, 67–69
variability of demand, 62–65

L

Lead time, 2, 23, 30, 37, 43–45, 52, 56, 60,
    62, 66, 67, 74, 78, 79

M

M&A, *see* Mergers and acquisitions (M&A)
Management strategy, 65–67
Market segmentation, 43
    high-growth, 19–24, 26
    types of, 16–18, 24–25, 35, 42, 43–47,
        52, 54, 62, 64
Materials requirement planning (MRP), 44
Mergers and acquisitions (M&A), 1
MRP, *see* Materials requirement planning
    (MRP)

O

On-time delivery, 23, 44, 45, 67–69, 73

P

P&L, *see* Profit and loss (P&L)
Payment terms, 46, 47, 70, 72–73, 75, 78, 79
Product line, 18, 20–21, 25, 27–28, 31, 35, 36
Profit and loss (P&L), 1, 2, 59

R

Ready-to-use door market segment, 17, 18,
    25, 27, 33, 35
Requests for quote (RFQs), 7
Research in Motion (RIM), 1
Return on invested capital (ROIC), 59, 70,
    77–78, 87–88
Revenue growth, 15–32
    compounded annual growth rate
        (CAGR), 16
    custom doors, 16
    inorganic, 15
    organic, 15
    pricing, 26–32
        average selling price (ASP), 26
        eliminating unfavorable outliers,
            26–28

execution, 30–32
new products, 30
products for value, 28–30
profitable, 15
ready to use, 17
semicustom doors, 17
standard doors, 17
volume, 19–26
    current performance to meet needs,
        23–24
    develop action plan, 24–26
    identify high-growth market
        segments, 19–21
    needs of the high-growth market
        segments, 21–23
RFQs, *see* Requests for quote (RFQs)
RIM, *see* Research in Motion (RIM)
ROIC, *see* Return on invested capital
    (ROIC)

S

Selling, general, administrative (SG&A)
    costs, 36, 41, 53–54
Semicustom door market segment, 17, 18,
    21, 22–25, 28–29, 32, 33, 35, 37,
    43, 45–47, 52, 54, 63–64, 72, 74
SG&A, *see* Selling, general, administrative
    (SG&A)
Standard door market segment, 17, 18, 25,
    27, 33, 35, 42, 43, 47, 61
Stocking levels, 67–69

V

Value-based pricing, 28, 30, 32, 37
Variability of demand, 62–65
VOC, *see* Voice of the customer (VOC)
Voice of the customer (VOC), 21, 22, 23,
    36, 44, 45, 54

W

Working capital, 56, 59–76
    inventory, 60–69
        levels over time, 61–62
        management strategy, 65–67
        stocking levels, 67–69
        variability of demand, 62–65
    return on invested capital (ROIC), 59